LEARN
Italian
in a Hurry

GRASP
THE BASICS OF
Italiano
Rapidamente!

Michael P. San Filippo

Aadamsmedia
Avon, Massachusetts

Published by
Adams Media, an F+W Publications Company
57 Littlefield Street, Avon, MA 02322
www.adamsmedia.com

ISBN 10: 1-59869-550-9
ISBN 13: 978-1-59869-550-2

Printed in Canada.

J I H G F E D C B A

Library of Congress Cataloging-in-Publication Data
San Filippo, Michael.
Learn Italian in a hurry / Michael San Filippo.
p. cm.
ISBN-13: 978-1-59869-550-2 (pbk.)
ISBN-10: 1-59869-550-9 (pbk.)
1. Italian language—Textbooks for foreign speakers—English.
2. Italian language—Self-instruction. I. Title.
PC1129.E5S265 2007
458.2'421—dc22   2007019007

This publication is designed to provide accurate and authoritative information
with regard to the subject matter covered. It is sold with the understanding
that the publisher is not engaged in rendering legal, accounting, or other
professional advice. If legal advice or other expert assistance is required, the
services of a competent professional person should be sought.
—From a *Declaration of Principles* jointly adopted by a Committee of the
American Bar Association and a Committee of Publishers and Associations

Many of the designations used by manufacturers and sellers to distinguish
their product are claimed as trademarks. Where those designations appear in
this book and Adams Media was aware of a trademark claim, the designations have been printed with initial capital letters.

Contains materials adopted and abridged from *The Everything® Learning
Italian Book,* by Michael San Filippo, Copyright © 2003 by F+W
Publications, Inc.

This book is available at quantity discounts for bulk purchases.
For information, please call 1-800-289-0963.

Contents

Introduction

We live in an era of E-ZPass highway lanes, instant messaging, and even microwave pizza. In the spirit of these hyperactive times, then, here are some great ways to speak Italian quickly and effectively while *divertendoti* (amusing yourself).

Go to Italian-speaking places: You've always wanted to visit your grandmother's hometown in Sicily. And that travel guide description of the Pompeii ruins left you breathless. The fastest way to speak Italian is to travel to Italy and submerge yourself in the language. If you visit Italy not only will you get to see Roman ruins, Renaissance masterpieces, and Raffaello's paintings, but you'll also learn how to roll your *rrr*s!

Listen to radio and TV: One of the key skills in language acquisition is comprehending the spoken language. Nowadays many cable companies broadcast at least an hour a day of Italian programming, typically a news feed from RAI, the state television channel. In addition, there are many Italian radio stations that can be accessed via the Internet such as Radio Marte.

Use stickers: Learning a language requires creativity—so why not try something that will amuse your family and friends! Grab a pad of self-stick notes and write the Italian word for everything in your house—plaster your kitchen, living room, garage—even the *gatto*! Whenever you see the sticker, say the name aloud until it becomes automatic. It's a terrific way to increase your vocabulary.

No matter what method you prefer, remember to bring along this book, *Learn Italian in a Hurry*. There's a key to pronunciation so you can learn your ABCs (open wide and say *ahh*!), and a vocabulary guide with hundreds of definitions. There are essential Italian phrases to help expand your word power and tables to conjugate verbs *pronto*. And there are sections on the essentials, such as telling time, greeting people, and asking for directions. It's all arranged to help you develop a foundation for advancing quickly in the language, and designed to make learning Italian fun and easy!

01 / Beginning Italian

Learn Your ABCs and How to Pronounce Them

Twenty-one letters is all it takes to produce the sweet, lyrical language affectionately called *la bella lingua* (the beautiful language). Using the Roman alphabet and with the addition of acute and grave accents (which will be explained later in this chapter), native Italian speakers are able to argue passionately about their favorite soccer team, discuss the latest elections, or order gnocchi genovese while sounding like characters in a Verdi opera.

What happened to the other five letters that are common in other languages using the Roman alphabet? They're found in foreign words that have infiltrated Italian, and are pronounced approximately as they are in the original language.

▶ The Italian Alphabet

Letter	Italian Name	Italian Example	Approximate English Sound
a	a	arancia, ape	father, car
b	bi	bagno, buono	beer, barrel, bark

Italian Letter	Italian Name	Italian Example	Approximate English Sound
c	ci	cane, cosa, ciao, cedro	cane, care, church, chest
d	di	donna, denaro	dim, dank, duck
e	e	essere, edicola	bet, met, set
f	effe	fango, furbo	farce, fill, firm
g	gi	grazie, gamba, gentilezza, gente	go, gab, gem, general
h	acca	che, hai	(this letter is silent)
i	i	idea, isola	police, cheese, these
l	elle	libro, lento	loud, lark, lamb
m	emme	mamma, mago	math, music, march
n	enne	nano, Natale	number, name, nail
o	o	otto, occhio	bold, sold, rote
p	pi	prego, Pasqua	party, pay, pill
q	qu	quadro, questo	quiet, queen, quandary
r	erre	riso, ragno	rain, run, rag (but roll those Italian rs!)
s	esse	strega, stanza	slam, steal, smog
t	ti	topo, terra	tear, time, tongue
u	u	uomo, uno	croon, noon, root
v	vu	vino, volcano	vase, valley, vine
z	zeta	zio, zaino	reds, nets, sets

▶ Foreign Letters

Letter	Italian Name	Example
j	i lungo, i lunga	jolly, jazz
k	cappa	kimono, poker
w	doppia vu, vu dopio	sandwich, welter
x	ics	box, unisex
y	ipsilion, i greco	sexy, yoga

For help in spelling and pronouncing words in Italian, here's a simple rule: What you hear is what you get. Italian is a phonetic language, which means most words are pronounced as they are written. The Italian words *cane*, *mane*, and *pane* will always rhyme (compare the English triplet "chalice," "police," and "lice," and you will see that you've got it easy). Another point to keep in mind is enunciation. Native Italian speakers open their mouths wide—not just to shout, but to get those big, round, vowel sounds. For example, if you want to pronounce the Italian letter *a*, just open wide and say "aahh!"

Consonants and Vowels

Italian pronunciation might pose some difficulties for the beginner. Yet it is very regular, and once the rules are understood it is easy to pronounce each word correctly. As you can see from the next table, most Italian consonants are similar in pronunciation to their English counterparts. The consonants *c* and *g* are the only exceptions, because they vary according to the letters that follow them. Here are a few basic pronunciation rules for these two consonants:

- When *c* appears before *e* or *i*, it sounds like "ch" in the English word "church." In the contraction *c'è* (there is), pronounced "cheh," the letter *c* also has the same "soft c" sound. In all other cases, it has a sound similar to the English "k."
- When *g* appears before *e* or *i*, it sounds like "g" in the English word "general." When it appears before *n*, it sounds like the "ny" in "canyon." When it appears in the combination *gli*, it sounds like "ll" in the English word "million." In all other cases, it has a sound like the "g" in "good."

Double the Consonants, Double the Fun

In Italian, double consonants are pronounced much more forcefully than single consonants. Although it may not be obvious at first, a trained ear will notice the difference. Make it a point to listen to native speakers pronounce these words.

Any consonant except *h* can be doubled. With double *f, l, m, n, r, s,* and *v,* the sound is prolonged; with double *b, c, d, g, p,* and *t,* the stop is stronger than for the single consonant. Double *z* is pronounced almost the same as single *z.* Double *s* is always unvoiced—in other words, spoken as a single *s.*

▶ Common Single and Double-Consonant Words

Italian	English	Italian	English
cane	dog	canne	canes
casa	house	cassa	trunk
copia	copy	coppia	couple
dona	gift	donna	woman
nono	ninth	nonno	grandfather
pala	shovel	palla	ball
papa	pope	pappa	bread soup
sera	evening	serra	greenhouse
tufo	tuff	tuffo	plunge
velo	veil	vello	pelt

Attenzione! Yes, there is a difference in the pronunciation between *penne* and *pene.* When you order a bowl of that flavorful tube-shaped pasta, the *cameriere* (waiter) may gently nudge you and repeat PEN-neh, pronouncing the *n* longer and more emphatically, to emphasize the correct word choice. (*Penne* refers to the fact that the pasta is shaped like quills. *Pene* is the Italian word for "penis.")

I'd Like to Buy a Vowel Please

Italian vowels are short, clear cut, and are never drawn out—the "glide" with which English vowels frequently end should be avoided. It should be noted that *a, i,* and *u* are always pronounced the same way; *e* and *o,* on the other hand, have an open and a closed sound that may vary from one part of Italy to the other.

- Open *e* in *cello, lento,* and *è* sounds like the English "met."
- Closed *e* in *sete, bene, pepe,* and *vede* sounds like the English "cake."
- Open *o* in *cosa, costa,* and *donna* sounds like the English "cost."
- Closed *o* in *dopo, mondo, molto, dove,* and *sole* sounds like the English "bone."

When to Stress and When Not to Stress

Usually, the stress in Italian words falls on the next-to-last syllable. A few typical words that follow this general rule are listed in the table below.

▶ Words with Stress on the Next-to-Last Syllable

Italian	English	Italian	English
bistecca	steak	pilota	pilot
campagna	countryside	pizza	pizza
cervello	brain	pompelmo	grapefruit
insegnare	to teach	sorella	sister
patente	driver's license	studiare	to study

When the stress falls on the last syllable, the final vowel is accented—usually with a grave (downward-pointing) accent. The grave accent also appears in a few miscellaneous words. A few representative words with the grave accent on the last syllable are listed in the table below.

▶ **Words with Stress on the Last Syllable**

Italian	English	Italian	English
cioè	namely	più	more
città	city	università	university
già	already	venerdì	Friday
però	however	virtù	virtue

Grave and acute (upward-pointing) accent marks are also used with single-syllable words in order to distinguish them from others that have the same spelling but a different meaning.

▶ **Single-Syllable Words**

Italian	English	Italian	English
da	gives	ne	some
dà	from	né	nor
e	and	se	if
è	is	sé	himself, herself
la	the; it; her	si	oneself
là	there	sì	yes

Traditionally, the grave (downward-pointing) accent has been used on the accented final vowels *à* and *ò*, while the acute (upward-pointing) accent was placed on all other final vowels. Today, there is a growing trend to disregard this rule, especially in nonformal publications, and only use the grave accent: for instance, *perchè* instead of *perché*, or *anzichè* instead of *anziché*.

Punctuation

Now that you've learned your ABCs, you're probably dreaming of sitting in an olive grove, sipping Chianti, nibbling on pecorino cheese, and writing love poetry in Italian. Becoming the next Petrarca will take more than just fancy words and lots of passion. You'll need orthographic marks and punctuation too! Orthography is the representation of the sounds of a language by written or printed symbols, usually accent marks. Punctuation marks are those dots, dashes, and squiggles that denote pauses, questions, and other patterns of speech. While you may not use all of these on a regular basis, being able to refer to them in Italian will get you that much closer to captivating your Laura (Petrarca's heartthrob and the lucky recipient of his 365 love poems, one for every day of the year). Refer to the following table for a list of *segni d'interpunzione* (punctuation marks).

▶ **Punctuations Marks**

Mark	Name
,	la virgola
( )	le parentesi tonde
.	il punto; punto fermo
[ ]	le parentesi quadre
;	il punto e virgola
}	le sgraffe
:	due punti
*	l'asterisco
. . .	i puntini di sospensione
´	l'accento acuto (upward-pointing accent)
`	l'accento grave (downward-pointing accent)
?	il punto interrogativo
!	il punto esclamativo

▶ Punctuations Marks (continued)

Mark	Name
'	l'apostrofo
-	il trattino
/	la sbarretta
—	la lineetta
" "	le virgolette

Numbers and Counting

You might find cardinal (counting) numbers the most useful to know—you will need them to express time, record dates, do math, interpret recipe amounts, and, of course, count. In Italian, cardinal numbers are written as one word. Use the following table to memorize numbers from 1 to 100.

▶ Italian Cardinal Numbers 1–100

Number	Name	Pronunciation
1	uno	OO-noh
2	due	DOO-eh
3	tre	TREH
4	quattro	KWAHT-troh
5	cinque	CHEEN-kweh
6	sei	SEH-ee
7	sette	SET-teh
8	otto	OHT-toh
9	nove	NOH-veh
10	dieci	dee-EH-chee
11	undici	OON-dee-chee
12	dodici	DOH-dee-chee
13	tredici	TREH-dee-chee
14	quattordici	kwaht-TOR-dee-chee
15	quindici	KWEEN-dee-chee

Number	Name	Pronunciation
16	sedici	SEH-dee-chee
17	diciassette	dee-chahs-SET-teh
18	diciotto	dee-CHOHT-toh
19	diciannove	dee-chahn-NOH-veh
20	venti	VEN-tee
21	ventuno	ven-TOO-noh
22	ventidue	ven-tee-DOO-eh
23	ventitré	ven-tee-TREH
24	ventiquattro	ven-tee-KWAHT-troh
25	venticinque	ven-tee-CHEEN-kweh
26	ventisei	ven-tee-SEH-ee
27	ventisette	ven-tee-SET-teh
28	ventotto	ven-TOHT-toh
29	ventinove	ven-tee-NOH-veh
30	trenta	TREN-tah
40	quaranta	kwah-RAHN-tah
50	cinquanta	cheen-KWAHN-tah
60	sessanta	ses-SAHN-tah
70	settanta	set-TAHN-ta
80	ottanta	oht-TAHN-ta
90	novanta	noh-VAHN-tah
100	cento	CHEN-toh

The numbers *venti*, *trenta*, *quaranta*, *cinquanta*, and so on drop the final vowel when combined with *uno* and *otto*. *Tre* is written without an accent, but *ventitré*, *trentatré*, and so on do require an accent mark.

Beyond 100

Do you remember those good old days before the euro's arrival in Italy when you would pay a few thousand lire for a cappuccino and biscotti? Tourists needed more than just the numbers up to 100 to get around.

Lire are history, but learning numbers greater than 100 might still prove useful. Though they might seem unwieldy, after a bit of practice you'll be rolling them off your tongue like a pro.

▶ **Italian Cardinal Numbers: 100 and Greater**

Number	Name	Pronunciation
100	cento	CHEN-toh
101	centouno/centuno	cheh-toh-OO-noh/chehn-TOO-noh
150	centocinquanta	cheh-toh-cheen-KWAHN-tah
200	duecento	doo-eh-CHEN-toh
300	trecento	treh-CHEN-toh
400	quattrocento	kwaht-troh-CHEN-toh
500	cinquecento	cheen-kweh-CHEN-toh
600	seicento	seh-ee-CHEN-toh
700	settecento	set-teh-CHEN-toh
800	ottocento	oht-toh-CHEN-toh
900	novecento	noh-veh-CHEN-toh
1.000	mille	MEEL-leh
1.001	milleuno	meel-leh-OO-noh
1.200	milleduecento	meel-leh-doo-eh-CHEN-toh
2.000	duemila	doo-eh-MEE-lah
10.000	diecimila	dee-eh-chee-MEE-lah
15.000	quindicimila	kween-dee-chee-MEE-lah
100.000	centomila	chen-toh-mee-leh
1.000.000	un milione	OON mee-lee-OH-neh
2.000.000	due milioni	DOO-eh mee-lee-OH-neh
1.000.000.000	un miliardo	OON mee-lee-ARE-doh

Did you notice? When Italians write down numbers as digits, they use the period to denote breaks between thousands, and the comma to indicate the decimal point—the exact opposite of what you're used to doing in English.

Ordinal Numbers

You can place items in "order" with ordinal numbers. For instance, *il primo* is the first course on a menu and *il secondo* is the second course. Vittorio Emanuele III, who ruled the unified Italian nation from 1900 to 1946, was the third king with that name. Pope Paul V (1605–1621) was the fifth pope with the name Paul. When used with the numerical succession of kings, popes, and emperors, the ordinal numbers are capitalized:

- Vittorio Emanuele Secondo (Vittorio Emanuele II)
- Leone Nono (Leone IX)
- Carlo Quinto (Carlo V)
- *diciottesimo secolo* (eighteenth century)

▶ **Italian Ordinal Numbers**

English	Italian
first	primo
second	secondo
third	terzo
fourth	quarto
fifth	quinto
sixth	sesto
seventh	settimo
eighth	ottavo
ninth	nono
tenth	decimo
eleventh	undicesimo
twelfth	dodicesimo
thirteenth	tredicesimo
fourteenth	quattordicesimo
fifteenth	quindicesimo
sixteenth	sedicesimo
seventeenth	diciassettesimo

English	Italian
eighteenth	diciottesimo
nineteenth	diciannovesimo
twentieth	ventesimo
twenty-first	ventunesimo
twenty-third	ventitreesimo
hundredth	centesimo
thousandth	millesimo
two thousandth	duemillesimo
three thousandth	tremillesimo
one millionth	milionesimo

Notice the regularity of ordinal numbers beginning with *undicesimo*—the suffix *–esimo* is added to the cardinal numbers by dropping the final vowel of the cardinal number. The one exception includes numbers ending in *–tré*. Those numbers drop their accent and are unchanged when *–esimo* is added. Since Italian ordinal numbers function as adjectives, they must agree in gender and number with the nouns they modify: *primo, prima, primi, prime*.

Italian in English, English in Italian

Italian words have been migrating to English over the course of many centuries. Most musicians are familiar with terms such as bel canto, cello, mezzosoprano, pianoforte, and solo. Architecture has borrowed words like cupola, loggia, and stanza. If you like Italian food, there's no avoiding mouth-watering ravioli, mozzarella, lasagne, vermicelli, or porcini. And in everyday culture we speak of camera-toting paparazzi, graffiti artists, gun-slinging mafia, and the urban ghetto. So your vocabulary already consists of many familiar words that are Italian. *Figuriamoci!* (Imagine that!)

Because of the growing influence of American culture, especially through the media, it's a two-way linguistic street. So many English words have been adopted in Italian that there's a name for them: *Itangliano* (highly anglicized Italian). These words include "club," "flirt," "shopping," "spray," and "style." It might seem as if you hear more English than Italian spoken in the tourist-heavy cities of Florence, Rome, and Venice!

The Best Way to Learn Italian

The Italian national soccer team, known as *gli Azzurri* because of the blue of their jerseys, has for years ranked among the top teams in the world. They've won the World Cup four times, Italian-born players routinely sign multi-million-dollar contracts for European teams, and the Italian soccer leagues offer some of the most talented competition anywhere. The overriding reason for their success? Practice, practice, practice. And that's the secret to learning Italian or any other foreign language. Exercise your language muscles every day, and soon you too will be competing with the best of them.

The quickest and most effective way to learn Italian is the total-immersion method. This means traveling to Italy for an extended period, studying at any of the thousands of schools throughout the country, and speaking only Italian. Many programs include a home-stay component that enhances the cultural exchange. You literally eat, breathe, and dream in Italian.

Unfortunately, not everyone has the opportunity to spend weeks or months in Florence, Rome, or other Italian towns sipping espresso, touring ancient ruins, and taking language classes. There are other ways to learn Italian without leaving your hometown, wherever that may be.

You've already taken the most important step to learning Italian when you picked up this book, because the most important thing is to start studying! And any method is appropriate, whether it's reading an Italian textbook, taking a language course online, at a university or local language school, completing workbook exercises, listening to a podcast, tape or CD, or conversing with a native Italian speaker. Spend some time every day reading, writing, speaking, and listening to Italian to become accustomed to the target language. Slowly but surely, your confidence will build, your vocabulary will expand, and you'll be communicating in Italian. Maybe you'll even start talking with your hands!

02 / Building Your Vocabulary

Greetings and Goodbyes

One of the best ways to practice your Italian is by greeting others on the street. Italians appreciate any attempt by others to speak their language, so go ahead and make the first move. Ingratiate yourself with the friendly sayings listed below.

▶ Italian Greetings

Italian	English
Salve!	Hello!
Pronto!	Hello! (when answering the phone)
Ciao!	Hi! (also: Bye!)
Buon giorno!	Good morning!
Buon pomeriggio!	Good afternoon!
Buona sera!	Good evening!
Come sta?	How are you?
Come va?	How're you doing?
Ci sentiamo bene.	We're feeling fine.
Grazie, va bene così.	Thanks, just fine.

Hello, My Name Is . . .

Unless you wear a name tag (definitely not the fashion in Italy), you'll also have to introduce yourself. If your name has an Italian equivalent, be bold and act the part too.

▶ Common English First Names and Their Italian Counterparts

English Name	Common Italian Translation	English Name	Common Italian Translation
Alexandra	Alessandra	Mark	Marco
Ann	Anna	Mary	Maria
Elizabeth	Elisabeta	Michael	Michele
Helen	Elena	Nicholas	Nicola
Joan	Giovanna	Patricia	Patrizia
John	Giovanni	Philip	Filippo
Joseph	Giuseppe	Theresa	Teresa
Katherine	Caterina	Thomas	Tommaso
Louis	Luigi	Vincent	Vincenzo
Luke	Luca		

Below, you will find some common ways of introducing yourself.

▶ Introductions

Italian	English
Mi chiamo Michele.	My name is Michael.
Piacere di conoscerLa.	Pleased to meet you. (formal form)
Questa è mia moglie.	This is my wife.
Questo è mio marito.	This is my husband.
Come si chiama?	What is your name?
Di dov'è?	Where are you from?
Dove lavora?	Where do you work?
Che cosa studia?	What are you studying?
Lei abita qui?	Do you live here?

Note that in Italian—as in other Romance languages—there is a formal and an informal form of address. Later in this book, you'll learn more about this!

Mark Your Calendars

Here are some points worth mentioning about the Italian calendar: The Italian week begins on Monday. The days of the week, the names of the seasons, and the names of months are not capitalized in Italian. And, finally, there is an explanation for why *settembre* (September) is the "seventh" month, *ottobre* (October) is the "eighth," *novembre* (November) is the "ninth," and *dicembre* (December) is the "tenth": A very long time ago, the Roman calendar began in March, so September, October, November, and December were the seventh, eighth, ninth, and tenth months of the year. For a complete list of months (*i mesi*), refer to the table below.

▶ **Months of the Year**

Italian	English	Italian	English
gennaio	January	luglio	July
febbraio	February	agosto	August
marzo	March	settembre	September
aprile	April	ottobre	October
maggio	May	novembre	November
giugno	June	dicembre	December

Another bit of trivia: When a religious festival or holiday falls on a Tuesday or Thursday, Italians oftentimes *fare il ponte*, or make a four-day holiday, by taking off the intervening Monday or Friday. To learn Italian days of the week (*giorni della settimana*), take a look at the table below.

▶ Days of the Week

Italian	English
lunedì	Monday
martedì	Tuesday
mercoledì	Wednesday
giovedì	Thursday
venerdì	Friday
sabato	Saturday
domenica	Sunday

Here are a few other phrases you might find useful:

- Che giorno è oggi? (What day is it today?)
- Oggi è martedì. (Today is Tuesday.)
- Domani è mercoledì. (Tomorrow is Wednesday.)
- Ieri è stato lunedì. (Yesterday was Monday.)

Closed for the Holidays

One thing to remember if you visit Italy: Check the calendar. Not only are there holidays that are part of the government calendar, but many towns and cities celebrate saints' days and local festivals. The tourist board should have this information available, but here are the country's official national holidays, when everything shuts down—including museums, public buildings, and many retail shops.

▶ National Holidays in Italy

Date	Italian Holiday	English Translation
January 1	Capodanno	New Year's Day
January 6	Epifania	Feast of the Epiphany
Easter Monday	Pasquetta	Little Easter
April 25	Festa della Resistenza	Liberation Day
May 1	Festa dei Lavoratori	Labor Day

Date	Italian Holiday	English Translation
August 15	Ferragosto	Feast of the Assumption
November 1	Ognissanti	All Saints' Day
December 8	Immacolata Concezione	Immaculate Conception
		of the Blessed Virgin Mary
December 25	Natale	Christmas
December 26	Festa di Santo Stefano	St. Stephen's Day

Telling Time

You've got to know the time if you want to see those Botticelli paintings at the Uffizi in Florence. Luckily, there are two ways to ask "What time is it?" in Italian: *Che ora è?* and *Che ore sono?* If the time is one o'clock, noon, or midnight, the answer is in the singular; for all other hours, it is plural. Note that the phrase "o'clock" has no direct equivalent in Italian.

- Che ora è? (What time is it?)
- Che ore sono? (What time is it?)
- È l'una. (It's one o'clock.)
- È mezzogiorno. (It's noon.)
- È mezzanotte. (It's midnight.)
- Sono le tre e quindici. (It's 3:15.)
- È mezzo giorno e dieci. (It's 12:10.)

▶ Common Terms Related to Telling Time

English	Italian
noon	mezzogiorno
half past	e mezzo
a quarter to/before	meno un quarto
morning	di mattino
evening	di sera

English	Italian
midnight	mezzanotte
a quarter	un quarto
a quarter after/past	e un quarto
afternoon	del pomeriggio
sharp	in punto

Store hours, TV timetables, performance listings, and other time references are written differently in Italy. When telling time, commas replace colons. For example, 2:00 becomes 2,00; 2:30 becomes 2,30; 2:50 becomes 2,50.

Take a look at the following table to see how you would tell the time from 5:00 to 6:00.

▶ **Telling Time: 5:00–6:00**

Time	Italian Way of Saying It
5,00	Sono le cinque.
5,10	Sono le cinque e dieci.
5,15	Sono le cinque e un quarto.
5,20	Sono le cinque e venti.
5,30	Sono le cinque e mezzo.
5,40	Sono le sei meno venti.
5,45	Sono le sei meno un quarto.
5,50	Sono le sei meno dieci.
6,00	Sono le sei.

As in most of Europe, Italy uses the so-called "official time" (equivalent to "military time" in the United States) in train schedules, performances, movie timetables, radio, TV, and office hours. Between friends and in other informal situations, Italians may use the numbers from 1 to 12 to indicate time, and the context of the conversation will usually be sufficient. After all, La Scala doesn't have performances at eight in the morning!

The Family

The Italian family is one of the most enduring strengths of Italian culture. Even today, with increased mobility due to cars, airplanes, and other modes of transportation, many Italians prefer to live in the same town that they grew up in, raise their own family in familiar surroundings, and cheer on the same hometown soccer team that they've rooted for since childhood.

This cultural trait makes for very strong community bonds and traditions, and for strong family bonds as well. For vocabulary of *la famiglia* (the family), see the following table.

▶ **Family Vocabulary**

English	Italian
brother	il fratello
brother-in-law	il cognato
daughter	la figlia
family	la famiglia
father	il padre
father-in-law	il suocero
grandchild	il/la nipote (di nonni)
grandfather	il nonno
grandmother	la nonna
husband	il marito
mother	la madre
mother-in-law	la suocera
nephew/niece	il/la nipote (di zii)
parents	i genitori
relative	il parente
sister	la sorella
son	il figlio
uncle	lo zio
wife	la moglie

Describing Things and People

Italian and English differ in their usage of adjectives. Italian descriptive adjectives are usually placed after the noun they modify, and with which they agree in gender and number. (When you learn a new adjective, it will be presented to you in the masculine singular form.)

▶ Common Adjectives Ending in –o

Italian	English	Italian	English
allegro	cheerful, happy	buono	good, kind
cattivo	bad, wicked	freddo	cold
grasso	fat	leggero	light
nuovo	new	pieno	full
stretto	narrow	timido	timid, shy

Adjectives ending in –o have four forms: masculine singular, masculine plural, feminine singular, and feminine plural. Observe how the adjectives *nero* and *cattivo* change to agree with nouns they modify.

▶ Endings of –o Adjectives

Singular	Plural
il gatto nero (the black cat, masculine)	i gatti neri (the black cats, masculine)
la gatta nera (the black cat, feminine)	le gatte nere (the black cats, feminine)

Singular	Plural
il ragazzo cattivo (the bad boy)	i ragazzi cattivi (the bad boys)
la ragazza cattiva (the bad girl)	le ragazze cattive (the bad girls)

Note that when an adjective modifies two nouns of different gender, it retains its masculine ending. For example: *i padri e le madre italiani* (Italian fathers and mothers).

Non –O Endings

Not all Italian adjectives have a singular form ending in *–o*. There are a number of adjectives that end in *–e*. The singular ending *–e* changes to *–i* in the plural, whether the noun is masculine or feminine.

▶ **Ending of –e Adjectives**

Singular	Plural
il ragazzo triste (the sad boy)	i ragazzi tristi (the sad boys)
la ragazza triste (the sad girl)	le ragazze tristi (the sad girls)

▶ **Adjectives Ending in –e**

Italian	English	Italian	English
abile	able	difficile	difficult
facile	easy	felice	happy
forte	strong	grande	big, large, great
importante	important	intelligente	intelligent
interessante	interesting	triste	sad
veloce	fast, speedy		

There are quite a few other exceptions for forming plural adjectives. For instance, adjectives that end in *–io* (with the stress falling on that *i*) form the plural with the ending *–ii: addio/addii; leggio/leggii; zio/zii.*

The following table contains a chart of other irregular adjective endings you should know.

▶ **Forming Plural Adjectives**

Singular Ending	Plural Ending	Singular Ending	Plural Ending
–ca	–che	–co	–chi
–cia	–ce	–ga	–ghe
–cio	–ci	–gia	–ge

Singular Ending	Plural Ending	Singular Ending	Plural Ending
—gia	—ge	—go	—ghi
—gio	—gi	—scia	—sce
—glia	—glie	—scio	—sci
—glio	—gli		

Following the Order

As you have already seen, adjectives generally follow the noun:

- È una lingua difficile. (It is a difficult language.)
- Marina è una ragazza generosa. (Marina is a generous girl.)

Certain common adjectives, however, generally come before the noun:

- Anna è una cara amica. (Anna is a dear friend.)
- Gino è un bravo dottore. (Gino is a good doctor.)
- È un brutt'affare. (It's a bad situation.)

The most common adjectives that come before the noun are listed below.

▶ Adjectives the Precede Nouns

Italian	English	Italian	English
bello	beautiful	bravo	good, able
brutto	ugly	buono	good
caro	dear	cattivo	bad
giovane	young	grande	large, great
lungo	long	nuovo	new
piccolo	small, little	stesso	same
vecchio	old	vero	true

But even these adjectives must follow the noun for emphasis or contrast, and when modified by an adverb:

- Oggi non porta l'abito vecchio, porta un abito nuovo. (Today he is not wearing the old suit, he is wearing a new suit.)
- Abitano in una casa molto piccola. (They live in a very small house.)

03 / Grammar

Maybe you fell in love with the rolling hills of Tuscany on your first visit to *il bel paese*—or maybe you fell in love with an Italian! Maybe your grandparents emigrated from Italy, so you want to investigate your family history. Perhaps you're an aspiring musician who wants to learn what *adagio*, *allegro*, and *andante* mean, or an opera singer who wants to improve her pronunciation. For all these reasons and more, you've decided to learn Italian, improve on what lessons you've already taken, or formalize those rudimentary phrases you've been speaking when traveling to Italy.

No matter what your motivation—-the opportunity to work overseas, cultural exchange in a land steeped in history and culture, researching your genealogy, or studying other topics such as literature or art history—you can discover new worlds when learning Italian. So raise a glass of Montepulciano and congratulate yourself on embarking on a new adventure. *Buon viaggio!*

Top Ten Reasons to Learn Italian

1. Understand Luciano Pavarotti when he belts out a phrase in a high C.
2. Order in Italian with confidence at an authentic Italian restaurant.
3. Improve your cultural understanding and global communication.
4. Stop relying on subtitles when watching Italian-language movies.
5. Get directions in Italian on your next visit to Rome.
6. Converse with your Italian-born grandparents.
7. Choose the right size at the Armani boutique in Florence without guessing.
8. Research your family roots and interpret old documents.
9. Study art history in the land where Michelangelo was born.
10. Read *La Divina Commedia* as Dante wrote it.

Love Those Romance Languages!

What comes to mind when you hear the word "romance"? Champagne and chocolates, candlelight dinners, soft music, and Valentine's Day? Not many people will think Italian, Spanish, or Portuguese. So what are Romance languages and why is Italian part of this group?

Linguistically speaking, Romance languages are descendants of the spoken form of Latin, known as Vulgar Latin. In this case, "vulgar" doesn't mean "coarse" or "off-color," but rather "common," referring to the usual, typical, everyday speech of ordinary people.

Romance languages consist of modern French, Italian, Spanish, Romanian, Catalan, the Romansch group of dialects (spoken in Switzerland), and Sardinian. Also included are such languages as Occitan and Provençal (France), Andalusian (Spain), Friulian (northeast Italy), Ladin (northern Italy), and Sicilian (southern Italy).

Many Romance languages are regional dialects rather than national languages, classified together on the basis of a shared section of vocabulary, which originated from the influence of the language of the Roman conquerors on the local native languages spoken in the Mediterranean area (where the Romance languages are clustered). Today, nearly 400 million people speak Romance languages.

Italian, like the other Romance languages, is the direct offspring of the Latin spoken by the Romans and imposed by them on the peoples under their dominion. Of all the major Romance languages, Italian retains the closest resemblance to Latin.

Blueprint of a Sentence

I eat pizza. Sicily is a large island. Gina feels well. In English, sentence structure is straightforward. Usually, it's noun, verb, object (direct or indirect). In Italian, though, sentence structure is much more flexible. Sometimes the noun follows the verb for emphasis or for rhythm: *Lui è strano* and *È strano lui* mean the same thing: "He is strange." Sometimes, the object precedes the verb—that is, when it's a direct or indirect object pronoun. *Non la mangia.* (He doesn't eat it.) *Perché non li inviti?* (Why don't you invite them?)

In fact, there are several verbs in Italian—including *piacere, bastare, dispiacere, mancare, occorrere,* and *servire*—that have the following sentence structure: indirect object + verb + subject. It's not your usual sentence structure, but in the case of *piacere* (to please, to like) and the other verbs listed, that's the way it works in Italian, and here's why: In English, you say that A likes B. In Italian, though, the same meaning is understood in different terms: B pleases A. Key word: different. Italian isn't English and vice versa. That's just the way it is. In the case of the verb *mancare*, "*Mi manchi*" means "You are missing (*manchi*) to me (*a me*, or *mi*—indirect object)."

Person, Place, or Thing

You've heard it since grade school: What's a noun? A person, place, or thing. Nouns (*i nome*) are one of the first things that people learn, whether it's their native or second language. *Bicchiere, vino, funghi.* Glass, wine, mushrooms. And in Italian, what's noticeable almost immediately is that nouns have endings that change depending on the gender. The next table includes a few nouns to start with.

▶ **Italian Nouns**

Masculine	Feminine
banco (school desk)	cartella (book bag)
libro (book)	lavagna (chalkboard)
ragazzo (boy)	ragazza (girl)
specchio (mirror)	scuola (school)
zaino (backpack)	material (subject)
zio (uncle)	zia (aunt)

Most Italian nouns end in a vowel—those that end in a consonant are of foreign origin—and all nouns have a gender, even those that refer to qualities, ideas, and things. Usually, Italian singular masculine nouns end in –*o*, while feminine nouns end in –*a*. There are exceptions, of course.

▶ Italian Nouns Ending in –e

Masculine	Feminine
giornale (newspaper)	frase (sentence)
mare (sea)	nave (ship)
nome (name)	notte (night)
pane (bread)	classe (class)
ponte (bridge)	canzone (song)

All nouns ending in *–amma* are masculine, while all nouns ending in *–zione* are feminine. Almost all nouns ending in *–ore, –ere, –ame, –ale, –ile*, and a consonant + *–one* are masculine: *il pittore, il cameriere, lo sciame, l'animale, il porcile, il bastone.*

Two Pizze and a Bowl of Spaghetti

Sometimes one pizza just isn't enough—and one glass of red wine isn't sufficient to quench your thirst. When forming the plural of Italian nouns, the vowel endings change to indicate a change in number. For regular masculine nouns that end in *–o*, the ending changes to *–i* in the plural.

▶ Plural Forms of Masculine Nouns Ending in –o

Singular	Plural	English
fratello	fratelli	brothers
libro	libri	books
nonno	nonni	grandfather
ragazzo	ragazzi	boys
vino	vini	wine

Regular feminine nouns that end in *–a* take on *–e* endings in the plural.

▶ Plural Forms of Feminine Nouns Ending in –*a*

Singular	Plural	English
casa	case	houses
penna	penne	pens
pizza	pizze	pizza
ragazza	ragazze	girls
sorella	sorelle	sisters

When forming the plural of nouns ending in a consonant, such as words of foreign origin, only the article changes: *il film/i film*. Here are some exceptions to the rule for forming feminine plurals:

- Feminine-noun ending –ea changes to –ee in the plural. For example: *dea/dee* (goddess/goddesses).
- Feminine-noun ending –ca changes to –che in the plural. For example: *amica/amiche* (friend/friends). Remember that –che is pronounced as "keh" in Italian.

Finally, recall that some nouns end in –*e*. The plural forms of these nouns will end in –*i* (regardless of gender).

▶ Plural Forms of Nouns Ending in –*e*

Singular	Plural	English
bicchiere	bicchieri	(wine) glass
chiave	chiavi	keys
fiume	fiumi	rivers
frase	frasi	phrases
padre	padri	fathers

Articles: Definite and Indefinite

The English indefinite articles "a" and "an" correspond to the Italian *un*, *uno*, *un'*, and *una*, which are used with singular nouns. Take a look at the table below for examples.

▶ **Singular Indefinite Articles**

Masculine	Feminine
un amico (a friend)	una casa (a house)
un libro (a book)	una lezione (a lesson)
uno sbaglio (a mistake)	un'automobile (a car)
uno zio (an uncle)	un'università (a university)

In Italian, the form of the *l'articolo indeterminativo* (indefinite article) is dependent on the initial sound of the noun it precedes. *Uno* is used for masculine words beginning with *z, ps,* or *gn*, or with *s* + consonant; *un* is used for all other masculine words. The feminine form *una* becomes *un'* before a word that begins with a vowel (to avoid awkward pronunciation).

The Word "The"—Seven Different Ways

In English, the definite article has only one form: "the." In Italian, *l'articolo determinativo* has different forms according to the gender, number, and first letter of the noun or adjective it precedes.

Take a look at these examples:

- il libro e la matita (the book and the pencil)
- i ragazzi e le ragazze (the boys and girls)
- la Coca-Cola e l'aranciata (the Coke and orangeade)
- gli italiani e i giapponesi (the Italians and the Japanese)
- le zie e gli zii (the aunts and uncles)
- *Lo* (*gli* in plural) is used before masculine nouns beginning with *s* + consonant or with *z*.

- *Il* (*i* in plural) is used before masculine nouns beginning with all other consonants.
- *L'* (*gli* in plural) is used before masculine nouns beginning with a vowel.
- *La* (*le* in plural) is used before feminine nouns beginning with a consonant.
- *L'* (*le* in plural) is used before feminine nouns beginning with a vowel.

The article agrees in gender and number with the noun it modifies and is repeated before each noun. The first letter of the word immediately following the article determines the form of the article. Compare and contrast the pairs below.

▶ **Use Definite Articles with Nouns and Adjectives**

Italian	English
il giorno	the day
lo zio	the uncle
i ragazzi	the boys
l'amica	the girlfriend
l'altro giorno	the other day
il vecchio zio	the old uncle
gli stessi ragazzi	the same boys
la nuova amica	the new girlfriend

In Italian, the definite article must always be used before the name of a language, except when the verbs *parlare* (to speak) or *studiare* (to study) directly precede the name of the language—in those cases, the use of the article is optional:

- Studio l'italiano. (I study Italian.)
- Parlo italiano. (I speak Italian.)

■ Parlo bene l'italiano. (I speak Italian well.)

The definite article is also used before the days of the week to indicate a repeated, habitual activity. For example:

■ Domenica studio. (I'm studying on Sunday.)
■ Marco non studia mai la domenica. (Marco never studies on Sundays.)

Unlike English, the Italian definite article must be used with all general or abstract nouns.

Family Is Special

Mom and dad, your brothers and sisters, grandpa and your Aunt Millie. They're all special people, and so there's a rule just for them.

In the plural form, the definite article will appear before the possessive adjective that refers to a family member or relative. For example, instead of saying "my brothers," you are literally saying "the my brothers." The following table contains other examples.

▶ **Use of Definite Articles with Possessive Adjectives**

Italian	English
Mio fratello è carino.	My brother is cute.
I miei fratelli sono carini.	My brothers are cute.
Questo è mio zio.	This is my uncle.
Questi sono i miei zii.	These are my uncles.
Mia nonna è vecchia.	My grandmother is old.
Le mie nonne sono vecchie.	My grandmothers are old.
Mio cugino è straordinario.	My cousin is exceptional.
I miei cugini sono straordinari.	My cousins are exceptional.

Two Essential Verbs: *Essere* and *Avere*

Language means action, and you can't speak Italian without the verbs *essere* (to be) and *avere* (to have). These two essential verbs are used in compound verb formations, idiomatic expressions, and many other grammatical constructions. Become the maestro of these two verbs and you'll have taken a giant step toward learning Italian.

To Be or Not to Be: Essere

As the English verb "to be," *essere* is used in myriad grammatical and linguistic situations. Learning the many conjugations and uses of the verb is crucial to the study of the Italian language.

- La bambina è piccola. (The child is small.)
- Chi è? Sono io. Siamo noi. (Who is it? It's me. It's us.)
- Che ore sono? Sono le quattro. (What time is it? It is four o'clock.)

Essere is an irregular verb (*un verbo irregolare*); it does not follow a predictable pattern of conjugation (see the following table). Note that the form *sono* is used with both *io* (I) and *loro* (they). The context of the sentence will usually make evident the correct meaning.

▶ **Conjugating *Essere* (To Be)**

Person	Singular	Plural
I	(io) sono (I am)	(noi) siamo (we are)
II	(tu) sei (you are, familiar)	(voi) siete (you are, familiar)
III	(Lei) è (you are, formal)	(Loro) sono (you are, formal)
III	(lui/lei) è (he/she is)	(loro) sono (they are)

The expression *c'è* means "there is," and *ci sono* means "there are." These expressions are used to indicate where somebody or something is located:

■ C'è una chiesa. (There is a church.)
■ Ci sono due chiese. (There are two churches.)

The word *ecco* also means "here is/here are" or "there is/there are," but is used to draw attention to or point out something. For example: *Ecco Stefano!* (Here is Stefano!)

All-Purpose Verb

You'll soon realize that the verb *essere* is an all-purpose grammatical tool that's indispensable in a variety of situations. Here are a few examples of how *essere* is used in Italian:

■ *Essere* is used with *di* + name of a city to indicate city of origin (the city someone is from). To indicate country of origin, an adjective of nationality is generally used:
■ Io sono di Napoli. Tu di dove sei? (I'm from Naples. Where are you from?)
■ È cinese. (She is Chinese.)

■ *Essere* + *di* + proper name indicates possession. Italian does not use the "apostrophe + s" constructions that English speakers rely on to signal possession.
■ È di Giovanna. (It is Giovanna's. Literally: It is of Giovanna.)
■ Questa chitarra è di Beppino; non è di Vittoria. (This guitar is Beppino's; it's not Vittoria's.)

- To find out who owns something, ask *Di chi è* . . . ?
- Di chi è questo libro? (Whose book is this?)
- Di chi sono questi libri? (Whose books are these?)

Essere is also used as an auxiliary verb in the following cases:

1. Reflexive verbs: Those verbs whose action reverts to the subject, as in the following examples: I wash myself. Mi lavo. They enjoy themselves. Si divertono.
2. Impersonal form: As in general statements in English that rely on one of the following subjects: "one," "you," "we," "they," or "people" + verb. For example: Si mangia bene in Italia. (People/they eat well in Italy.)
3. Passive voice: In a passive construction the subject of the verb receives the action instead of doing it, as in the sentence: Caesar was killed by Brutus. Cesare è stato ucciso da Brutus.

Essere is not just a verb though! It can be used as a noun to mean "being," "individual," or "existence": *un essere fortunato* is a lucky fellow; *essere umano* is a human being; *essere razionale* is a rational being.

To Have or Not to Have: Avere

Like the verb *essere*, *avere* is used in a variety of ways. After learning the conjugations and uses of the verb, you'll be that much closer to understanding the Italian language. Take a look at a few of these examples to see how *avere* works in an Italian sentence:

- Ho molti amici. (I have many friends.)
- Ha una villa in campagna. (He has a house in the country.)
- Maria ha un vestito nuovo. (Maria has on a new dress.)

Avere is an irregular verb (*un verbo irregolare*); it does not follow a predictable pattern of conjugation. Even though most forms of *avere* begin with *h*, that letter is never pronounced. Commit to memory the present tense (*il presente*) form of *avere* (see the following table)—you will see it in many Italian grammatical constructions.

▶ Conjugating *Avere* (To Have)

Person	Singular	Plural
I	(io) ho (I have)	(noi) abbiamo (we have)
II	(tu) hai (you have, familiar)	(voi) avete (you have, familiar)
III	(Lei) ha (you have, formal)	(Loro) hanno (you have, formal)
III	(lui/lei) ha (he/she has)	(loro) hanno (they have)

Idiomatic Expressions with *Avere*

Espressioni idiomatiche, or idiomatic expressions, are phrases that have a special meaning in context. The verb *avere* is used in many idiomatic expressions to convey feelings or sensations and take the form *avere* + noun. In English these expressions are usually formed with "to be" + adjective. The next table contains some common idiomatic expressions using *avere*.

▶ **Idiomatic Expressions with *Avere***

Italian	*English*
avere bisogno di	to need, have need of
avere caldo	to be warm (hot)
avere fame	to be hungry
avere freddo	to be cold
avere fretta	to be in a hurry
avere paura	to be afraid
avere sete	be thirsty
avere sonno	to be sleepy
avere voglia di	to want, to feel like
avere a che fare con	to deal with
avercela con	to have it in for
aversela a male	to feel bad

Here is how you might use these expressions in a sentence:

▪ Michele ha sempre fretta. (Michael is always in a hurry.)

▪ Ho caldo. Ho voglia di un gelato. (I'm hot. I feel like having ice cream.)

▪ Non capisco proprio perché ce l'hai con me. (I really don't understand why you have it in for me.)

▪ È inutile che io le parli; vuole avere a che fare solo con te. (It's no use my talking to her; she only wants to deal with you.)

▪ Non avertela a male se non ti invito a quella cena. Ho già troppi invitati. (Don't feel bad if I don't invite you to that dinner. I have too many guests already.)

How Old Are You?

The verb *avere* is also used in discussing age: *avere* + [number] + *anni* means "to be [number] years old":

- Quanti anni hai? (How old are you?)
- Ho trentuno anni. (I'm thirty one.)
- Questa gatta è vecchia, ha quindici anni. (This cat is old, it is fifteen years old.)

Transitive Verbs and Using Avere

The compound tenses (*i tempi composti*) are verb tenses that consist of two words, such as the *passato prossimo* (present perfect). Both the verbs *essere* and *avere* act as helping verbs in compound tense formations. For example: *io sono stato* (I was) and *ho avuto* (I had). Now you know why *avere* and *essere* are so important!

Present Perfect with *Avere*

In general, transitive verbs (verbs that carry over an action from the subject to the direct object) are conjugated with *avere* as in the following example:

- Il pilota ha pilotato l'aeroplano. (The pilot flew the plane.)

When the *passato prossimo* is constructed with *avere*, the past participle does not change according to gender or number:

- Io ho parlato con Giorgio ieri pomeriggio. (I spoke to George yesterday afternoon.)
- Noi abbiamo comprato molte cose. (We bought many things.)

When the past participle of a verb conjugated with *avere* is preceded by the third person direct object pronouns *lo, la, le,* or *li,* the past participle agrees with the preceding direct object pronoun in gender and number. The past participle may agree with the direct object pronouns *mi, ti, ci,* and *vi* when these precede the verb, but the agreement is not mandatory.

- Ho bevuto la birra. (I drank the beer.)
- L'ho bevuta. (I drank it.)
- Ho comprato il sale e il pepe. (I bought the salt and pepper.)
- Ci hanno visto/visti. (They saw us.)

In negative sentences, *non* is placed before the auxiliary verb:

- Molti non hanno pagato. (Many didn't pay.)
- No, non ho ordinato una pizza. (No, I didn't order a pizza.)

For a more detailed look at past participles, keep reading!

Present Perfect with *Essere*

When *essere* is used, the past participle always agrees in gender and number with the subject of the verb. In many cases, intransitive verbs (those that cannot take a direct object), especially those expressing motion, are conjugated with the auxiliary verb *essere.* The verb *essere* is also conjugated with itself as the auxiliary verb. Some of the most common verbs that form compound tenses with *essere* are listed below.

▶ Intransitive Verbs that Appear with *Essere* in Present Perfect

Italian	*English*
andare	to go
arrivare	to arrive
cadere	to fall
dimagrire	to diet
entrare	to enter
immigrare	to immigrate
morire	to die
partire	to depart
restare	to stay, to remain
(ri)tornare	to return
salpare	to weigh anchor
sfuggire	to run away to, to set sail, to flee
stare	to stay, to be
uscire	to go out
venire	to come

First-Conjugation Verbs (*–are* Verbs)

Verbs are fundamental to any language, and Italian is no exception. There are three primary groups of verbs, and this chapter will deal with the first-conjugation group, those Italian verbs that end in *–are*. Most Italian verbs belong to the first-conjugation group and follow a highly uniform pattern. Once you learn how to conjugate one *–are* verb, you've essentially learned hundreds of them.

It's Time to Conjugate

The infinitives of all regular verbs in Italian end in *–are*, *–ere*, or *–ire* and are referred to as first-, second-, or third-conjugation verbs, respectively. In English, the infinitive (*l'infinito*) consists of "to" + verb. The present tense (*il tempo presente*) is a simple tense—that is, the verb form consists of one word only.

Regular Verbs

The present tense of a regular *–are* verb is formed by dropping the infinitive ending *–are* and adding the appropriate endings to the resulting stem *(–o, –i, –a, –iamo, –ate, –ano)*. See the table below for a sample conjugation of *amare* (to love).

▶ **Conjugations of the Verb *Amare* (To Love)**

Person	Singular	Plural
I	(io) amo (I love)	(noi) amiamo (we love)
II	(tu) ami (you love, familiar)	(voi) amate (you love, familiar)
III	(Lei) ama (you love, formal)	(Loro) amano (you love, formal)
III	(lui/lei) ama (he/she loves)	(loro) amano (they love)

The infinitive of first-conjugation Italian verbs (those ending in *–are*) and the conjugated forms of the present tense are pronounced like most Italian words: The stress falls on the next-to-last syllable. The one exception is the third-person plural form *amano,* which is pronounced AH-mah-noh, with stress falling on the first syllable. Other first-conjugation verbs are listed in below.

▶ **First-Conjugation Verbs**

Italian	English
arrivare	to arrive
ascoltare	to listen
aspettare	to wait

Italian	English
ballare	to dance
camminare	to walk
cantare	to sing
dimenticare	to forget
guidare	to drive
imparare	to learn
insegnare	to teach
lavorare	to work
parlare	to speak
pranzare	to dine, to have lunch
nuotare	to swim
suonare	to play (an instrument)
telefonare	to telephone
visitare	to visit

Irregular First-Conjugation Verbs

While the endings of most Italian verbs of the first conjugation follow the regular pattern you just learned, there are a few exceptions with regard to spelling. As you'll see, most of the time, spelling irregularities are introduced in order to maintain the consonant sound that precedes the endings.

Verbs Ending in –care and –gare

When you conjugate verbs ending in –care (*giocare*, *caricare*) and –gare (*litigare*, *legare*), add an *h* immediately after the root in the *tu* and *noi* forms to maintain the hard *c* or hard *g* sound of the infinitive. For an example of this structure, see the conjugation of *giocare* (to play) on the next page.

▶ Conjugating *Giocare* (To Play)

Person	Singular	Plural
I	(io) gioco	(noi) giochiamo
II	(tu) giochi	(voi) giocate
III	(lui, lei, Lei) gioca	(loro, Loro) giocano

Other verbs that end in *–care* or *–gare* are listed here.

allargare	to widen
attaccare	to attack, to glue
divagare	to amuse
impaccare	to pack
pagare	to pay
toccare	to touch
allungare	to lengthen
cercare	to search for
frugare	to rummage
indagare	to investigate
sbarcare	to disembark
troncare	to break, to cut off

Verbs Ending in *–ciare, –giare,* and *–sciare*

When you conjugate verbs ending in *–ciare* (*cominci-are*), *–giare* (*mangiare*), or *–sciare* (*lasciare*), drop the *i* of the root in the *tu* and *noi* forms before adding the regular endings (in order to avoid the unusual combination *ii,* which is rare in the middle of words). For an example, look at how to conjugate *mangiare.*

▶ Conjugating *Mangiare* (To Eat)

Person	Singular	Plural
I	(io) mangio	(noi) mangiamo
II	(tu) mangi	(voi) mangiate
III	(lui, lei, Lei) mangia	(loro, Loro) mangiano

There are quite a few other verbs in this category. See a list below.

assaggiare	to taste
cominciare	to start
invecchiare	to grow old, to age
noleggiare	to rent...a car, etc.
parcheggiare	to park
racconciare	to fix, to mend
strisciare	to creep, to crawl
viaggiare	to travel

Verbs Ending in –*iare*

With verbs ending in –*iare* (*inviare, studiare, gonfiare*), the *i* of the root is dropped when the accent is on the next-to-last syllable in the first person singular of the present indicative (*io invio*)—see table below for a complete conjugation of *avviare* (to direct, to send).

▶ **Conjugating *Avviare* (To Direct, To Send)**

Person	Singular	Plural
I	(io) avvio	(noi) avviamo
II	(tu) avvii	(voi) avviate
III	(lui, lei, Lei) avvia	(loro, Loro) avviano

Other verbs that may be included in this category appear below.

cambiare	to change
gonfiare	to inflate
inviare	to dispatch, to forward
rinviare	to send back, to return

spiare   to spy on, to watch
studiare   to study

Verbs Ending in *–gliare* and *–gnare*

Verbs ending in *–gliare* (*tagliare*, *pigliare*) drop the *i* of the root only before the vowel *i*. To see a sample conjugation, refer to the table here.

▶ Conjugating *Tagliare* (to Cut)

Person	Singular	Plural
I	(io) taglio	(noi) tagliamo
II	(tu) tagli	(voi) tagliate
III	(lui, lei, Lei) taglia	(loro, Loro) tagliono

Other verbs that belong to this category are listed here.

aggrovigliare   to entangle
avvinghiare   to clutch, to grip
pigliare   to take
regnare   to rule, to reign
sbagliare   to mistake, to err
sognare   to dream

Three's a Crowd

So far, you've learned irregular verbs that undergo spelling changes for reasons of pronunciation. However, there are three first-conjugation verbs that are irregular in their stem as well as some of the endings. They include *dare* (to give), *stare* (to stay), and *andare* (to go)—the following three tables will help you see this.

▶ Conjugating *Dare* (To Give)

Person	Singular	Plural
I	(io) do	(noi) diamo
II	(tu) dai	(voi) date
III	(lui, lei, Lei) dà	(loro, Loro) danno

▶ Conjugating *Stare* (To Stay)

Person	Singular	Plural
I	(io) sto	(noi) stiamo
II	(tu) stai	(voi) state
III	(lui, lei, Lei) sta	(loro, Loro) stanno

▶ Conjugating *Andare* (To Go)

Person	Singular	Plural
I	(io) vado	(noi) andiamo
II	(tu) vai	(voi) andate
III	(lui, lei, Lei) va	(loro, Loro) vanno

You might think that the irregular verb *fare* (to do, to make) should also belong here, but it belongs to the second-conjugation category, because it is derived from the Latin verb *facere*, a second-conjugation verb.

The Scoop on *Andare*

In Italian, the sequence of *andare* + *a* + infinitive is equivalent to the English "to go" + infinitive (to go dancing, to go eat, and so on). Note that it is necessary to use *a* even if the infinitive is separated from the form of *andare*. For example:

■ Quando andiamo a ballare? (When are we going dancing?)

■ Chi va in Italia a studiare? (Who's going to Italy to study?)

Andare also works with various means of transportation—for instance, *andare in aeroplano* is literally "to go by airplane" (to fly). Note that in all of these expressions *andare* is followed by *in*, except in the expression *andare a piedi* (to walk). Here are a few additional examples:

■ andare in bicicletta (to ride a bicycle)
■ andare in treno (to go by train)
■ andare in automobile/in macchina (to drive, to go by car)

Here is an interesting rule: The phrase "go to" will translate as *andare in* when referring to countries, and *andare a* when referring to cities, so you would say *vado in Italia, a Roma* (I'm going to Italy, to Rome).

Like the verb *stare*, *andare* may be combined with other words to take on new meanings. Here are some of the most frequently used expressions with *andare*:

andare avanti	to proceed, to go on
andare con	to accompany, to take, to go with
andare dentro	to enter, to go in
andare fuori	to go out
andare indietro	to back up
andare lontano	to go far away
andare per terra	to fall
andarsene	to go away, to leave

Second-Conjugation Verbs (*–ere* Verbs)

Italian verbs with infinitives ending in *–ere* are called second-conjugation (*seconda coniugazione*) or *–ere* verbs. The present tense of a regular *–ere* verb is formed by dropping the infinitive ending and adding the appropriate endings (*–o, –i, –e, –iamo, –ete, –ono*) to the stem. For an example on how to conjugate a regular second-conjugation verb, take a look at the table below.

▶ Conjugating *Scrivere* (To Write)

Person	Singular	Plural
I	(io) scrivo	(noi) scriviamo
II	(tu) scrivi	(voi) scrivete
III	(lui, lei, Lei) scrive	(loro, Loro) scrivono

Second-conjugation (*–ere*) verbs account for approximately one quarter of all Italian verbs. Although many have some sort of irregular structure, there are also many regular verbs (see below) that are conjugated in the same way as *scrivere*.

accendere	to put out, extinguish
battere	to beat, to hit
cadere	to fall
chiedere	to ask
conoscere	to know
correre	to run
credere	to believe
descrivere	to describe
eleggere	to elect
leggere	to read
mettere	to put, to place
mordere	to bite
nascere	to be born

offendere	to offend
perdere	to lose
ridere	to laugh
rompere	to sell
rimanere	to break
sopravvivere	to survive
vendere	to remain, to stay

Irregular Second-Conjugation Verbs

Second-conjugation Italian verbs can give your mental spellchecker a vigorous workout. Here are just some of the many phonetic rules to be aware of.

Verbs Ending in *–gnere*

One example of these types of verbs are the ones ending in *–gnere*. Check them out below. Can you see what's irregular about it?

▶ Conjugating *Spegnere* (To Turn Off, To Put Out)

Person	Singular	Plural
I	(io) spengo	(noi) spegniamo
II	(tu) spegni	(voi) spegnete
III	(lui, lei, Lei) spegne	(loro, Loro) spengono

As you might have noticed, *spegnere* has two irregular forms: in the *io* and *loro/Loro* forms, where the soft *gn* switches to the hard *ng*.

Verbs Ending in *–cere*

Another verb group that undergoes a spelling modification includes verbs that end in *–cere*, like *dispiacere* (to displease). To see how this verb is conjugated, refer to the table on the next page.

▶ Conjugating *Dispiacere* (To Displease)

Person	Singular	Plural
I	(io) dispiaccio	(noi) dispiacciamo
II	(tu) dispiaci	(voi) dispiacete
III	(lui, lei, Lei) dispiace	(loro, Loro) dispiacciono

Some of the other verbs that belong to this category are listed here.

compiacere	to gratify, to please
giacere	to lie down
nuocere	to harm, to injure
piacere	to please
tacere	to be quiet

Verbs Ending in *–gliere*

Verbs in this category are very similar to verbs that end in *–gnere* (refer to the following table). That is, they undergo a spelling change in the *io* and *loro/Loro* forms, where two consonants switch places—in this case, from *gl* to *lg*. For example, take a look at the conjugation of *cogliere* (to pick, to pluck) here.

▶ Conjugating *Cogliere* (To Pick, To Pluck)

Person	Singular	Plural
I	(io) colgo	(noi) cogliamo
II	(tu) cogli	(voi) cogliete
III	(lui, lei, Lei) coglie	(loro, Loro) colgono

Some other verbs conjugated like *cogliere* are listed here.

accogliere	to give hospitality to, to welcome
raccogliere	to harvest, to gather

sciogliere	to undo, to untie, to loosen
togliere	to take off, to remove

Irregular: *Fare* and *Dire*

The verbs *fare* (to do, to make) and *dire* (to say, to tell) are considered second-conjugation verbs because they are derived from two Latin verbs of the second conjugation— *facere* and *dicere*, and do not follow the regular pattern of conjugation (infinitive stem + endings). See the tables below which conjugate *fare* and *dire* in the present tense.

▶ **Conjugating *Fare* (To Do, To Make)**

Person	Singular	Plural
I	(io) faccio	(noi) facciamo
II	(tu) fai	(voi) fate
III	(lui, lei, Lei) fa	(loro, Loro) fanno

▶ **Conjugating *Dire* (To Say, To Tell)**

Person	Singular	Plural
I	(io) dico	(noi) diciamo
II	(tu) dici	(voi) dite
III	(lui, lei, Lei) dice	(loro, Loro) dicono

Here is a list of some other verbs conjugated like *dire*.

benedire	to bless
contraddire	to contradict
disdire	to retract, to cancel
indire	to announce publicly, to declare
interdire	to prohibit
maledire	to curse

Verbs Ending in *–arre*, *–orre*, and *–urre*

Like *fare* and *dire*, verbs ending in *–arre* (*trarre*), *–orre* (*porre*), and *–urre* (*tradurre*) are considered second-conjugation verbs because they also derive from the contractions of Latin verbs (*trahere, ponere, traducere*). For the conjugation of *trarre* (to pull, to draw out), see below.

▶ **Conjugating *Trarre* (To Pull, To Draw Out)**

Person	Singular	Plural
I	(io) traggo	(noi) traiamo
II	(tu) trai	(voi) traete
III	(lui, lei, Lei) trae	(loro, Loro) traggono

Other verbs conjugated like *trarre* include *distrarre* (to distract), *contrarre* (to contract), and *sottrarre* (to subtract).

There are also quite a few verbs that end in *–orre*, the most common of which is, of course, *porre* (to place, to set down). The table below illustrates how to conjugate *porre* in the present tense.

▶ **Conjugating *Porre* (To Place, To Set Down)**

Person	Singular	Plural
I	(io) pongo	(noi) poniamo
II	(tu) poni	(voi) ponete
III	(lui, lei, Lei) pone	(loro, Loro) pongono

This list includes other verbs that end in *–orre*.

disporre	to arrange, to set out
esporre	to exhibit, to display
imporre	to impose

opporre	to oppose
posporre	to place or put after
proporre	to propose, to put
riporre	to put back, to replace
supporre	to suppose

Finally, you need to remember verbs that end in *–urre*, like *tradurre*. Let's take a look.

▶ Conjugating *Tradurre* (To Translate)

Person	Singular	Plural
I	(io) traduco	(noi) traduciamo
II	(tu) traduci	(voi) traducete
III	(lui, lei, Lei) traduce	(loro, Loro) traducono

Some other verbs conjugated like *tradurre* are listed below.

condurre	to take, to lead
introdurre	to introduce, to show
produrre	to produce, to yield
ridurre	to reduce, to curtail

Third-Conjugation Verbs (*–ire* Verbs)

If there are first-conjugation and second-conjugation verbs, then it stands to reason there are third-conjugation verbs (*terza coniugazione*)! This final group contains verbs that end in *–ire* in the infinitive. The present tense of a regular *–ire* verb is formed by dropping the infinitive ending and adding the appropriate endings (*–o, –i, –e, –iamo, –ite, –ono*) to the resulting stem. Note that, except for the *voi* form, these endings are the same as for regular second-conjugation (*–ere*) verbs. For an example of how to conjugate a regular *–ire* verb, see the table below, which conjugates *sentire* (to hear, to feel, to smell).

▶ Conjugating *Sentire* (To Hear, To Feel, To Smell)

Person	Singular	Plural
I	(io) sento	(noi) sentiamo
II	(tu) senti	(voi) sentite
III	(lui, lei, Lei) sente	(loro, Loro) sentono

Here are some other *–ire* third-conjugation regular verbs.

acconsentire	to agree, to acquiesce
aprire	to open
assorbire	to soak
bollire	to boil
coprire	to cover
cucire	to sew
dormire	to sleep
fuggire	to flee
mentire	to lie
morire	to die
offrire	to offer
partire	to leave
riaprire	to reopen
scoprire	to discover, to uncover
sequire	to follow
servire	to serve
sfuggire	to escape
soffrire	to suffer
vestire	to dress, to wear

A Special Case: –isc– Verbs

There is a special group of third-conjugation verbs that needs the suffix *–isc–* to be added to the stem of all three singular and the third-person plural forms. One good example of such verbs is *finire* (to finish). For a conjugation of *finire*, see below.

▶ **Conjugating *Finire* (To Finish)**

Person	Singular	Plural
I	(io) finisco	(noi) finiamo
II	(tu) finisci	(voi) finite
III	(lui, lei, Lei) finisce	(loro, Loro) finiscono

Most of the other verbs that need the *–isc–* suffix and are conjugated similar to *finire* are listed here. Unfortunately, there is no way to know which third-conjugation verbs are *–isc–* verbs. Your only option is to commit these verbs to memory.

capire	to understand
compatire	to commiserate with
conferire	to confer, to bestow
condire	to season, to flavor
contribuire	to contribute, to share in
dimagrire	to lose weight
impazzire	to go mad
inghiottire	to swallow up
istruire	to teach, to instruct
partire	to leave, to depart
preferire	to prefer
proibire	to forbid, to prohibit
pulire	to clean
reagire	to react
restituire	to return, to give back

ricostruire	to rebuild, to reconstruct
riferire	to relate, to refer
ristabilire	to re-establish, to restore
svanire	to disappear, to vanish
tossire	to cough
tradire	to betray, to be disloyal to
ubbidire	to obey

Negation

A sentence is usually made negative in Italian by placing the word *non* in front of the verb:

- Francesca vuole dormire. (Francesca wants to sleep.)
- Francesca non vuole dormire. (Francesca doesn't want to sleep.)
- Loro parlano cinese. (They speak Chinese.)
- Loro non parlano cinese. (They don't speak Chinese.)

Only object pronouns may be placed between *non* and the verb:

- Lo conosciamo. (We know him.)
- Non lo conosciamo. (We don't know him.)
- Lo hanno fatto. (They did it.)
- Non lo hanno fatto. (They did not do it.)

Two Negatives Make a Negative

Your grade school English teacher told you repeatedly that you couldn't use more than one negative word in the same sentence. In Italian, though, the double negative is the acceptable format, and even three negative words can be used in a sentence:

- Non viene nessuno. (No one is coming.)
- Non vogliamo niente/nulla. (We don't want anything.)
- Non ho mai visto nessuno in quella stanza. (I didn't see anyone in that room.)

In fact, there is a whole host of phrases made up of double (and triple) negatives. Here are most of them.

▶ **Double and Triple Negative Phrases**

Italian	English
non . . . nessuno	no one, nobody
non . . . affatto	not at all
non . . . niente	nothing
non . . . mica	not at all (in the least)
non . . . nulla	nothing
non . . . punto	not at all
on . . . né . . . né	neither . . . nor
non . . . neanche	not even
non . . . mai	never
non . . . nemmeno	not even
non . . . ancora	not yet
non . . . neppure	not even
non . . . più	no longer
non . . . che	only

Here are some examples of how these phrases may be used in Italian:

- Non ha mai letto niente. (She read nothing.)
- Non ho visto nessuna carta stradale. (I didn't see any street signs.)
- Non abbiamo trovato né le chiavi né il portafoglio. (We found neither the keys nor the wallet.)

Note that in the case of the negative expressions *non
. . . nessuno, non . . . niente, non . . . né . . . né*, and *non . . .
che*, the second part of the expression always follows the
past participle. Observe the following examples:

- Non ho trovato nessuno. (I haven't found anyone.)
- Non abbiamo detto niente. (We haven't said anything.)
- Non ha letto che due libri. (She has read only two
  books.)
- Non ho visto niente di interessante al cinema. (I didn't
  see anything of interest at the cinema.)

When using the combinations *non . . . mica* and *non
. . . punto, mica* and *punto* always come between the auxiliary verb and the past participle:

- Non avete mica parlato. (They haven't spoken at all.)
- Non è punto arrivata. (She hasn't arrived at all.)

When using the expressions *non . . . affatto* (not at
all), *non . . . ancora* (not yet), and *non . . . più* (no more,
no longer), the words *affatto, ancora*, or *più* can be placed
either between the auxiliary verb and the past participle
or after the past participle:

- Non è stato affatto vero. Non è affatto stato vero.
  (It wasn't true at all.)
- Non mi sono svegliato ancora. Non mi sono ancora
  svegliato. (I hadn't woken yet.)
- Non ho letto più. Non ho più letto. (I no longer read.)

Here you will find some negative phrases that you
should know!

▶ **Negative Phrases**

Italian	English
da niente	not important
mai	never
nessuno	no one, nobody
niente (nulla)	nothing
né . . . né	neither . . . nor
nessun	no, not . . . any
neanche, nemmeno, neppure	not even
per niente	at all

Note that *nessun* is used as an adjective, and must agree in gender and number with the thing that it describes. Moreover, *nessun* and *niente* usually follow the verb when they act as the object. When one of these words is the subject of the sentence, its position can vary:

■ Nessuno parla. (No one speaks.)
■ Niente ci piace. (We like nothing at all.)
■ Non parla nessuno. (No one speaks.)

The negative words *neanche*, *nemmeno*, and *neppure* are used to replace *anche* (too, also, as well) in negative sentences. Keep in mind that these three words can be used interchangeably, as in the following examples:

■ Non ha preso neanche il dolce. (He didn't even take the dessert.)
■ Nemmeno io ho visto nessuno. (I didn't see anyone either.)
■ Non leggiamo neppure i fumetti. (We don't even read the comic strips.)
■ Neanche loro lo so. (They don't know it either.)

Past Tense

The *passato prossimo*—referred to as the present perfect—is a compound tense (*tempo composto*) that expresses a fact or action that happened in the recent past or that occurred long ago but still has ties to the present.

Here are a few examples of how the *passato prossimo* appears in Italian:

- Ho appena chiamato. (I just called.)
- Mi sono iscritto all'università quattro anni fa. (I entered the university four years ago.)
- Questa mattina sono uscito presto. (This morning I left early.)
- Il Petrarca ha scritto sonetti immortali. (Petrarca wrote enduring sonnets.)

Now let's take a look at some adverbial expressions that are often used with the *passato prossimo*. These expressions usually indicate that the coinciding verb will be in the past tense.

▶ Common Adverbial Expression

Italian	English
ieri	yesterday
ieri pomeriggio	yesterday afternoon
ieri sera	last night
il mese scorso	last month
l'altro giorno	the other day
stamani	this morning
tre giorni fa	three days ago

Past Participles Are a Must!

Compound tenses such as the *passato prossimo* are formed with the present indicative of the auxiliary verb *avere* or *essere* and the past participle (*participio passato*). Now you know why you learned those two verbs first! The past participle of regular verbs is formed by dropping the infinitive ending *–are*, *–ere*, or *–ire* and adding the appropriate final ending: *–ato*, *–uto*, or *–ito*. Let's take a look.

▶ **Regular Past Participles of *–are* Verbs**

Infinitive Form	Past Participle
camminare (to walk)	camminato
imparare (to learn)	imparato
lavare (to wash)	lavato
telefonare (to telephone)	telefonato

▶ **Regular Past Participles of *–ere* Verbs**

Italian Verb	Past Participle
battere (to beat)	battuto
credere (to believe)	creduto
sapere (to know)	saputo
tenere (to keep)	tenuto

▶ **Regular Past Participles of *–ire* Verbs**

Italian Verb	Past Participle
capire (to understand)	capito
finire (to finish)	finito
gradire (to accept)	gradito
sentire (to feel, to smell)	sentito

The *passato prossimo* is often formed with a conjugated form of *avere*. To review, refer to the following table.

▶ *Passato Prossimo* with Regular Verbs

Person	Imparare (To Learn)	Credere (To Believe)	Capire (To Understand)
(io)	ho imparato	ho creduto	ho capito
(tu)	hai imparato	hai creduto	hai capito
(lui, lei, Lei)	ha imparato	ha creduto	ha capito
(noi)	abbiamo imparato	abbiamo creduto	abbiamo capito
(voi)	avete imparato	avete creduto	avete capito
(loro, Loro)	hanno imparato	hanno creduto	hanno capito

Irregular Past Participles

Many verbs in Italian, especially the *–ere* verbs, have irregular past participles. A list of some of the most common infinitives, along with a sample variation, as well as their past participle forms, appears here in the following table.

▶ Irregular Past Participles

Infinitive	Past Participle	Variation on the Infinitive	Past Participle
accendere	acceso	riaccendere	riacceso
chiedere	chiesto	richiedere	richiesto
chiudere	chiuso	racchiudere	racchiuso
cogliere	colto	raccogliere	raccolto
cuocere	cotto	stracuocere	stracotto
dire	detto	predire	predetto
dividere	diviso	condividere	condiviso
fare	fatto	strafare	strafatto
leggere	letto	rileggere	riletto
porre	posto	fraporre	fraposto

Past Infinitive	Variation on Participle	Past the Infinitive	Participle
reggere	retto	correggere	corretto
rispondere	risposto	corrispondere	corrisposto
rompere	rotto	corrompere	corrotto
scegliere	scelto	prescegliere	prescelto
scrivere	scritto	riscrivere	riscritto
trarre	tratto	ritrarre	ritratto
vincere	vinto	convincere	convinto
volgere	volto	rivolgere	rivolto

Build Your Vocabulary!

The irregular past participles of many groups of verbs have repeating patterns. For example, the past participle of any verb that ends in *–mettere* will also end in *–messo*:

- *ammettere*(to admit, to allow in, to let in)   *ammesso*
- *commettere* (to commit, to commission)   *commesso*
- *dimettere* (to dismiss, to remove)   *dimesso*
- *omettere* (to omit, to leave out)   *omesso*
- *rimettere* (to remit, to refer)   *rimesso*

Once you recognize the patterns, you'll be on your way to rapidly becoming an *esperto* of Italian verbs!

How to Choose the Auxiliary Verb

When forming the *passato prossimo*, which auxiliary verb should be used—*avere* or *essere*? How do you decide? As mentioned earlier in this chapter, compound tenses such as the *passato prossimo* are formed with the present indicative of the auxiliary verb *avere* or *essere* and the past participle (*participio passato*).

Transitive Verbs Take *Avere*

As you might remember from earlier in this chapter, transitive verbs are those that take a direct object. For instance:

- Io ho mangiato una pera. (I ate a pear.)
- Loro hanno già studiato la lezione. (They already studied the lesson.)
- Non ho mai visto Genoa. (I've never visited Genova.)

The compound tense of a transitive verb is formed with the present indicative of the auxiliary verb *avere* and the past participle (*participio passato*). The past participle is invariable and ends in *–ato, –uto,* or *–ito.* In phrases with a transitive verb, the direct object of the verb may be expressed explicitly or implied. For example: *Io ho mangiato tardi.* (I ate late.)

Intransitive Verbs Take *Essere*

Simply put, intransitive verbs are those that do not take a direct object. These verbs usually express movement or a state of being. The auxiliary verb *essere* plus the past participle is used to form the *passato prossimo* and other compounds of almost all intransitive verbs (and the past participle must agree in number and gender with the subject.)

The following table contains conjugations of *arrivare, crescere,* and *partire* in the *passato prossimo.*

▶ Passato Prossimo with *Essere*

Person	Arrivare (To Arrive)	Crescere (To Grow)	Partire (To Leave/Depart)
(io)	sono arrivato(–a)	sono cresciuto(–a)	sono partito(–a)
(tu)	sei arrivato(–a)	sei cresciuto(–a)	sei partito(–a)
(lui, lei, Lei)	è arrivato(–a)	è cresciuto(–a)	è partito(–a)

Person	Arrivare (To Arrive)	Crescere (To Grow)	Partire (To Leave/Depart)
(noi)	siamo arrivati(–e)	siamo cresciuti(–e)	siamo partiti(–e)
(voi)	siete arrivati(–e)	siete cresciuti(–e)	siete partiti(–e)
(loro, Loro)	sono arrivati(–e)	sono cresciuti(–e)	sono partiti(–e)

Notice that each of the past participles conjugated with *essere* has two possible endings, depending on the gender of its subject. Take a look at these examples:

- La zia è andata a casa. (The aunt went home.)
- Le zie sono andate a casa. (The aunts went home.)
- Lo zio è andato a casa. (The uncle went home.)
- Gli zii sono andati a casa. (The uncles went home.)

When the gender of the subject consists of both males and females, or is unstated, use the masculine form (think of it as a "generic" or "standard" form):

- Lo zio e la zia sono andati a casa. (The uncle and aunt went home.)
- Noi siami andati a casa. (We went home.)

The following table contains a list of other most commonly used intransitive verbs and their past-participle forms.

▶ Intransitive Verbs: Past Participles

Italian Verb	Past Participle
andare (to go)	andato
arrivare (to arrive, to reach)	arrivato
cadere (to fall, to drop)	caduto
costare (to cost)	costato

Italian Verb	*Past Participle*
crescere (to grow)	cresciuto
diventare (to become)	diventato
durare (to last, to continue)	durato
entrare (to enter)	entrato
essere (to be)	stato
morire (to die)	morto
nascere (to be born)	nato
partire (to leave)	partito
uscire (to exit)	uscito
venire (to come)	venuto

Some Verbs Take Either!

How could it be that some verbs take either *essere* or *avere* as the auxiliary verb in compound tenses? It depends on the context of the sentence. Here are a few examples of verbs functioning both transitively and intransitively:

Bruciare (to burn)
- Hai bruciato la torta? (Did you burn the cake?)
- Durante la notte scorsa la cascina è bruciata. (During the night, the dairy burned.)

Diminuire (to reduce, decrease)
- Abbiamo diminuito il consumo d'energia in casa. (We reduced energy consumption at home.)
- I prezzi della carne sono diminuiti questa settimana. (The price of meat has decreased this week.)

Finire (to finish)
- Il professore ha finito la conferenza alle tre. (The professor finished the conference at three o'clock.)

■ La conferenza è finita alle tre. (The conference finished at three o'clock.)

Agreeing on the Subject

Italians are all one big happy family, right? Maybe it's because there is so much cooperation in the Italian language. Plural nouns take plural articles, adjectives reflect the nouns they describe in both number and gender, and the past participles of verbs have a similar grammatical rule.

When using the conversational past or other compound tenses, the past participle of the acting verb must agree in gender and number with the direct-object pronoun preceding the verb *avere*. For example:

■ Hanno visitato il nonno. (They have visited their grandfather.)
BUT

■ Lo hanno visitato. (They have visited him. Also: L'hanno visitato.)

■ Ho comprato i pantaloni. (I have bought the pants.)
BUT

■ Li ho comprati. (I have bought them.)

■ Abbiamo veduto Teresa. (We have seen Theresa.)
BUT

■ L'abbiamo veduta. (We have seen her.)

■ Ha ricevuto le lettere. (He has received the letters.)
BUT

■ Le hai ricevute. (He has received them.)

Reflexive Verbs

You've already had a brief introduction to reflexive verbs, verbs that reflect upon themselves because their subject and object is one and the same person. When conjugating reflexive verbs in the *passato prossimo* or any other compound tense, you would use the auxiliary verb *essere* plus the past participle.

For the purposes of this chapter, observe the following examples:

- La ragazza si è guardata allo specchio. (The girl looked at herself in the mirror.)
- Il bambino si è addormentato. (The baby fell asleep.)
- Oggi mi sono alzato alle sei. (Today I got up at six.)

Future Tense

Tomorrow you will prepare pasta puttanesca. Saturday you will buy that Italian leather jacket you've been thinking about. Next year you will learn the future tense. *Che sarà, sarà*—what will be, will be! The future tense in Italian expresses an action that will take place in the future. Although in English the future is expressed with the helping verb "will" or the phrase "to be going to," in Italian a verb ending marks it as being set in the future tense. For example:

- Alla fine di settembre partirò per Roma. (At the end of September I will leave for Rome.)

First-Conjugation Verbs

The future tense (*futuro semplice*) of first-conjugation regular (*–are*) verbs is formed first by changing the infinitive ending *–are* into *–er* to obtain the root for the future tense. The following future endings are then added to the root: *–ò, –ai, à, –emo, –ete, –anno*. Let's look at the verb *cantare*, which means to sing.

▶ **Future Tense Conjugation of *Cantare***

Person	Singular	Plural
I	(io) canterò	(noi) canteremo
II	tu canterai	(voi) canterete
III	(lui, lei, Lei) canterà	(loro, Loro) canteranno

Second- and Third-Conjugation Verbs

The future tense of regular second- and third-conjugation (*–ere* and *–ire*) verbs is formed by simply dropping the final *–e* of the infinitive to obtain the stem and adding to the stem the following future endings: *–ò, –ai, –à, –emo, –ete, –anno* (the same endings, in fact, as those added to the first-conjugation group). For a sample conjugation, see the following table, which conjugates the verbs *credere*, to believe, and *partire*, to leave.

▶ **Future Tense Conjugations of *Credere* and *Partire***

Person	Singular	Plural
I	(io) crederò, partirò	(noi) crederemo, partiremo
II	tu crederai, partirai	voi crederete, partirete
III	(lui, lei, Lei) crederà, partirà	loro, Loro crederanno, partiranno

Future Tense of Irregular Verbs

In the future tense, the verbs *dare, stare,* and *fare* simply drop the final *–e* of their infinitives and form the stems *dar–, star–* and *far–*, respectively; the stem of *essere* is *sar–*. These stems are then combined with the regular future-tense endings.

The verbs listed in the following table also have an irregularly shortened stem in the future tense (usually, because the vowel *a* or *e* is dropped from the infinitive).

▶ Irregular Future-Tense Stems

Infinitive	Future Stem	Infinitive	Future Stem
andare	andr–	potere	potr–
avere	avr–	sapere	sapr–
cadere	cadr–	vedere	vedr–
dovere	dovr–	vivere	vivr–

Also be aware of the spelling of verbs with infinitives ending in *–ciare* and *–giare*. These verbs drop the *i* before adding the future endings to the root: *tu comincerai, noi viaggeremo*. Also, verbs with infinitives ending in *–care* and *–gare* add an *h* to the root for the future to preserve the hard sound of the *c or g* of the infinitive: *io cercherò, loro pagheranno*.

A Quick Look at the Subjunctive

Language is fluid, and usage changes. A case in point is the subjunctive (*il congiuntivo*), which in English is rapidly becoming extinct. Phrases like "I suggest you go home immediately" and "Robert wishes that you open the window" are not in frequent use anymore.

In Italian, though, the subjunctive tense is alive and flourishing, both in speaking and writing. Rather than stating facts, it expresses doubt, possibility, uncertainty, or personal feelings. It can also express emotion, desire, or suggestions. The following table provides examples of three regular verbs conjugated in the present subjunctive tense.

▶ Present Subjunctive

Pronoun	-are Verb parlare	-ere Verb scrivere	-ire Verbs sentire	capire
che io	parli	scriva	senta	capisca
che tu	parli	scriva	senta	capisca
che lui/lei/Lei	parli	scriva	senta	capisca
che noi	parliamo	scriviamo	sentiamo	capiamo
che voi	parliate	scriviate	sentiate	capiate
che loro/Loro	parlino	scrivano	sentano	capiscano

Typical phrases that call for the subjunctive tense include:

- Credo che . . . (I believe that . . .)
- Suppongo che . . . (I suppose that . . .)
- Immagino che . . . (I imagine that . . .)
- È necessario che . . . (It is necessary that . . .)
- Mi piace che . . . (I'd like that . . .)
- Non vale la pena che . . . (It's not worth it that . . .)
- Non suggerisco che . . . (I'm not suggesting that . . .)
- Può darsi che . . . (It's possible that . . .)
- Penso che . . . (I think that . . .)
- Non sono certo che . . . (I'm not sure that . . .)
- È probabile che . . . (It is probable that . . .)
- Ho l'impressione che . . . (I have the impression that . . .)

Certain verbs such as *suggerire* (to suggest), *sperare* (to hope), *desiderare* (to wish), and *insistere* (to insist) require use of the subjunctive too!

Conditional

Of course, as you've probably figured out by now, if there's a *congiuntivo presente*, there's a *congiuntivo passato* (present perfect subjunctive—and I don't ever remember my grade-school teacher using that term). And like other verb tense formations, the *congiuntivo passato* is a compound tense formed with the *congiuntivo presente* of the auxiliary verb *avere* or *essere* and the past participle of the acting verb.

▶ Congiuntivo Passato of the Verbs Avere and Essere

Pronoun	Avere	Essere
che io	abbia avuto	sia stato(–a)
che tu	abbia avuto	sia stato(–a)
che lui/lei/Lei	abbia avuto	sia stato(–a)
che noi	abbiamo avuto	siamo stati(–e)
che voi	abbiate avuto	siate stati(–e)
che loro/Loro	abbiano avuto	siano stati(–e)

Here are a few examples of the *congiuntivo passato*:

▪ Mi dispiace che abbia parlato così. (I'm sorry that he spoke that way.)
▪ Non credo che siano andati in Italia. (I don't believe they went to Italy.)

Prepositions

In English, you know them as "to," "in," "by," "on," "from," "for," and "since." In Italian, they are known as *a, in, da, di, con, in, per,* and *su,* among others. They are prepositions, those words that usually precede a noun or pronoun and express a relation to another word, as in the following simple sentences:

▪ The woman on the platform.
▪ They came after lunch.
▪ Why not go by bus?

Although there are general rules for the use of Italian prepositions, there's only one sure way to learn the correct usage: practice, practice, practice.

Mix and Match

When the prepositions *a, da, di, in,* and *su* are followed by a definite article, they are combined to form one word. The prepositional articles (*le preposizioni articolate*) take the forms listed here.

▶ **Prepositional Articles**

Definite Article	a	da	di	in	su
il	al	dal	del	nel	sul
lo	allo	dallo	dello	nello	sullo
l'	all'	dall'	dell'	nell'	sull'
i	ai	dai	dei	nei	sui
gli	agli	dagli	degli	negli	sugli
la	alla	dalla	della	nella	sulla
l'	all'	dall'	dell'	nell'	sull'
le	alle	dalle	delle	nelle	sulle

A: the All-Purpose Preposition

The preposition *a* can mean "to," "at," or "in," depending on how you use it in context. You will need the preposition *a* in the following cases:

1. To express the idea of going somewhere or staying somewhere (with names of cities):

■ Vado a Milano. (I go to Milan.)
■ Vado al mercato ogni lunedì. (I go to the market every Monday.)

- Si trova a Venezia. (It can be found in Venice.)
- Si trova alla piazza. (It can be found in the plaza.)

2. Before direct objects:

- Scriva a Rita. (He/she writes to Rita.)
- Scriviamo alla zia. (We write to our aunt.)
- Telefono agli amici. (They call their friends.)

3. The preposition a is also used with several verbs. Often those are verbs of motion, but in other instances it's a case of usage. That means either you'll have to commit them to memory, or, more likely, you'll grow accustomed to the usage over time as you listen and read Italian:

- andare a . . . (to go to)
- fermarsi a . . . (to stop)
- incoraggiare a . . . (to encourage)
- insegnare a . . . (to teach)
- invitare a . . . (to invite to)
- riuscire a . . . (to be careful)
- venire a . . . (to come to)

4. To form several grammatical constructions with particular significance:

- a mezzogiorno (at noontime)
- alle tre (at three)
- barca a vela (sailboat)
- sedia a rotelle (wheelchair)

In *Means "In"*

Usually the Italian preposition *in* means "in" in English, but it can also mean "to" or "by"! The preposition *in* is used in the following cases.

1. To express the idea of going somewhere or staying somewhere (with countries, continents, regions, large islands, and addresses):

- Vado in Italia. (I am going to Italy.)
- Vado nella Sicilia. (I am going to Sicily.)
- Abita in Germania. (He/she lives in Germany.)
- Roma è in Italia. (Rome is in Italy.)

2. In describing a method of transportation:

- Andiamo in macchina. (We are going by car.)
- Andiamo in autobus. (We are going by bus.)
- Viaggiamo in aereo. (We are traveling by plane.)
- Viaggiamo in barca. (We are traveling by boat.)

3. In dates, as a contraction *nel* (*in* + *il*):

- Cristoforo Colombo è nato nel 1451. (Christopher Columbus was born in 1451.)
- Caravaggio è morto nel 1570. (Caravaggio died in 1570.)

Da: *From Sea to Shining Sea*

The Italian preposition *da* means "from" in English. This preposition is used in time expressions, in which case you may translate it as "since" or "for." Italian uses the construction of present tense + *da* + time expressions to indicate an action that began in the past and is still going on in the present. For example:

- Da quanto tempo leggi questa rivista? (How long have you been reading this magazine?)
- Leggo questa rivista da molto tempo. (I've been reading this magazine for a long time.)

Da is also used in the following instances:

1. To express the equivalent of the English phrase "at the house of":

- Vado dal fratello. (I'm going to my brother's house.)
- Vado da Filippo. (I'm going to Filippo's house.)
- Andiamo dai signori Rossi. (We're going to the Rossi's house.)
- Andiamo da Gino. (We're going to Gino's house.)

2. To indicate origin or source:

- Vengo da Torino. (I come from Torino.)
- Vengo dalla Francia. (I come from France.)
- È tornato dalle vacanze. (He is back from vacation.)
- È tornato dagli zii. (He is back from his aunt and uncle's house.)

3. To indicate the worth or price of something:

- Voglio un francobollo da un'euro. (I want a 1 euro stamp.)
- È una casa da poco prezzo. (It's a house of little worth.)

Di: of the People

The Italian preposition *di* means "of" in English. It is used in the following cases:

1. To indicate possession:

- il libro di Maria (Maria's book)
- la padella del cuoco (the cook's pan)
- la casa dello zio (the uncle's house)

2. To indicate what an object is made of:

- il tavolo di legno (wooden table)
- la spada di metallo (metal knife)
- la medaglia di bronzo (bronze medal)

3. To indicate origin using the verb *essere + di + nome di città* (name of the city):

- Elisa è di Napoli. (Elisa is from Napoli.)
- Maurizio è di Prato. (Maurizio is from Prato.)
- I Rossi sono di Catania. (The Rossis are from Catania.)

4. The preposition *di* is used with certain verbs and adjectives:

- accorgersi di qualcosa (to notice something)
- innamorarsi di qualcuno (to be in love with someone)
- malato di una malattia (ill with a sickness)
- vergognarsi di qualcosa (to be ashamed by something)

5. The preposition *di* is found in many particular grammatical constructions:

- di sera (during the evening)
- di notte (at night)
- d'estate (during the summer)
- un uomo di mezza età (a man of middle age)

A Fearsome Foursome

The fearsome foursome of Italian prepositions are *per, su, con,* and *fra/tra*. The preposition *per* ("for" in English) is used to indicate the following:

1. Movement through space:

- Sono passati per Roma. (They passed through Rome.)
- Sono passati per Londra. (They passed through London.)

2. Duration of time:

- Ho lavorato per un anno intero. (I worked for an entire year.)
- Ho lavorato per due giorni senza una pausa. (I worked for two days without a break.)

3. Destination:

- Questa lettera è per il direttore. (This letter is for the director.)

Another useful preposition to know is *su* (on). *Su* is used in Italian to indicate location or a topic of discourse. For example:

- Il libro è sul tavolo. (The book is on the table.)
- Il cuscino è sul divano. (The cushion is on the couch.)
- È una conferenze sull'inquinamento industriale. (It is a conference on industrial pollution.)

The Italian preposition *con* is similar to the English "with":

- È uscito con la cugina. (He left with his cousin.)
- Sono andato con la mia famiglia. (I left with my family.)
- Taglia il pane con quel coltello. (He cuts the bread with that knife.)
- Apre la porta con questa chiave. (He/she opens the door with this key.)
- Ha risposto con gentilezza. (He/she responded with gentleness.)
- Lei ha gridato con gioa. (She screamed with joy.)

Finally, there is the preposition *tra* or *fra* (these words are fraternal twins and interchangeable in all cases), which may be used in the sense of "between" (whether between two locations, things, or people), or to indicate a time in the future with respect to the speaker. For example:

- Livorno è fra Roma e Genova. (Livorno is between Rome and Genoa.)
- Silvano è fra Maria e Davide. (Silvano is between Maria and David.)
- Fra qualche giorno arriverà la primavera. (In a few days spring will arrive.)
- Tra alcuni ore arriveremo. (In a few hours we'll arrive.)

04 / Putting It All Together

Express Yourself: Feeling Verbs

Now that you have the basics down, it is important that you are able to express yourself correctly! In order to do this, you should remember the helper verbs *potere* (to be able to, can), *volere* (to want), and *dovere* (to have to, must). But keep in mind that these verbs take on different meanings in different tenses. *Potere*, for example, can mean "to be able to," "can," "to succeed," "could," or "would be able to," depending on the context and tense. *Dovere* can mean "to owe," "to have to," "must," or "to be supposed to," according to the tense. Let's take a closer look at each.

Potere

In the present indicative tense, *potere* means "to be able to" or "can." For example:

- Posso uscire? (May I go out?)
- Posso suonare il trombone. (I can/am able to play the trombone.)

In the present perfect, *potere* means "to be able to, to succeed":

■ Ho potuto spedire il pacco. (I was able to mail the package.)
■ Non sono potuti venire più presto. (They could not come earlier, but they tried.)

In the conditional tenses (*condizionale presente* and *condizionale passato*), this verb may be translated as "could," "would be able to," "could have," or "could have been able to":

■ Potrei arrivare alle tre. (I was able to arrive at three o'clock—I would be able to arrive at three o'clock.)
■ Avrei potuto farlo facilmente. (I could have done it easily—I would have been able to do it easily.)

Volere
In the present indicative, *volere* means "want":

■ Voglio quell'automobile. (I want that car.)

In the present perfect (conversational past), *volere* is used in the sense of "decided, refused to":

■ Ho voluto farlo. (I wanted to do it—I decided to do it.)
■ Marco non ha voluto finirlo. (Mark didn't want to do it—Mark refused to do it.)

In the conditional, *volere* means "would like":

- Vorrei un bicchiere di latte. (I would like a glass of milk.)
- Vorrei visitare i nonni. (I would like to visit my grandparents.)

Dovere

The present indicative forms of *dovere* translate as "owe":

- Gli devo la mia gratitudine. (I owe him my gratitude.)
- Ti devo venti dollari. (I owe you twenty dollars.)

In the conditional tenses, however, *dovere* carries the meaning "should" or "ought to." For example:

- Dovrei finire i compiti di scuola a tempo. (I should/ought to finish my homework on time.)
- Avrei dovuto telefonarle immediatamente. (I should have/ought to have telephoned her immediately.)

Idiomatic Expressions

Espressioni idiomatiche, or idiomatic expressions, are phrases that have a special meaning in context. If *essere* is the Swiss army knife of verbs, then fare is the all-in-one, handy-dandy kitchen appliance. The verb fare expresses the basic idea of doing or making, as in *fare gli esercizi* (to do the exercises) and *fare il letto* (to make the bed), but it is also used in many idioms.

▶ **Idiomatic Expressions with *Fare***

Italian	*English*
fare alla romana	to split the check
fare castelli in aria	to daydream
fare colazione	to have breakfast
fare del proprio meglio	to do one's best
fare di tutto	to do everything possible
fare fingere	to pretend, make believe
fare forca	to play hooky
fare i compiti	to do one's homework
fare il biglietto	to purchase a ticket
fare il pieno	to fill up the gas tank
fare la fila/la coda	stand in line/wait in line
fare la spesa	to go grocery shopping
fare le spese	to go shopping
fare male	to be painful, to ache
fare passare	to let through
fare un capello in quattro	to split hairs
fare un viaggio	to take a trip
fare una domanda	to ask a question
fare una fotografia	to take a picture
fare una passeggiata	to take a walk
fare vedere	to show someone something
farsi coraggio	to take heart
farsi degli amici	to make friends
farsi in la	to step to one side
farsi la barba	to shave

Note that the infinitive *fare* is frequently abbreviated to *far* before a consonant. For example, you may say *far colazione, far male, far torto. Fare* is also used in many expressions relating to the weather (note that in the following translations, "it" is an impersonal subject and does not have an equivalent in Italian):

- Che tempo fa? (How is the weather?)
- Fa bel tempo. (The weather is nice.)
- Fa cattivo tempo. (The weather is bad.)
- Ha fatto caldo. (It has been warm.)
- Qui fa sempre freddo. (It's always cold here.)
- In primavera fa sempre fresco. (In spring it's always cool.)

Besides idiomatic expressions, and expressions relating to the weather, the verb *fare* is used in a number of proverbs:

- Chi la fa l'aspetti. (You will get as good as you gave.)
- Chi fa da sé fa per tre. (If you want something done, do it yourself.)
- Non fare agli altri ciò che non vorresti fosse fatto a te. (Do as you would be done by.)
- Tutto fa brodo. (Every little bit helps.)
- Chi non sa fare, non sa comandare. (A bad worker is a bad master.)

Commands

Many of the proverbs you just learned involved an imperative statement, or a command. Without the imperative, it would be difficult to advise your friends about what Italian towns to visit, the *forze armate* (armed forces) would cease to exist, and, most important, you'd no longer hear that famous phrase uttered by Italian mothers at the dinner table everywhere: *Mangia!* (Eat!)

Do Your Homework!

One of the most familiar figures in Mafia movies is that of *consigliere* (advisor, counselor). His role is to give advice to the head of the clan. And then, of course, the godfather gives the command to commit various nefarious acts—in the imperative, of course. The imperative verb forms are used to give orders or advice, to urge strongly, and to exhort. It is a simple tense—in the sense that it isn't compound—and has only one form, the present. Furthermore, you can address your command only to an informal form of "you": *tu* or *voi*, depending on whether you are talking to one or more people.

When conjugating a first-conjugation verb, the familiar singular (*tu*) command is the same as the third-person singular (*Lei*) form of the present indicative, and the plural *voi* command is the same as the *voi* form of the present indicative (see the table below).

▶ **First-Conjugation Verb Imperatives**

Infinitive	Tu	Voi
cantare	Canta!	Cantate!
mangiare	Mangia!	Mangiate!
parlare	Parla!	Parlate!

The familiar commands for regular *–ere* and *–ire* verbs are the same as the *tu* and *voi* forms of the present indicative.

▶ **Second- and Third-Conjugation Verb Imperatives**

Infinitive	Tu	Voi
dormire	Dormi!	Dormite!
finire	Finisci!	Finite!
pulire	Pulisci!	Pulite!
salire	Sali!	Salite!

scrivere	Scrivi!	Scrivete!
vendere	Vendi!	Vendete!

Listen to Me!

Although the imperative conjugation has a form you're already familiar with, there are some Italian verbs that have irregular forms for the familiar commands in the *tu* and *voi* forms.

▶ Irregular Imperatives

Infinitive	Tu	Voi
andare (to walk)	Va'!	Andate!
avere (to have)	Abbi!	Abbiate!
dare (to give)	Da'!	Date!
dire (to say, to tell)	Di'!	Dite!
essere (to be)	Sii!	Siate!
fare (to make)	Fa'!	Fate!
sapere (to know)	Sappi!	Sappiate!
stare (to stay)	Sta'!	State!

Negative Commands: Don't Touch That Dial!

We grew up hearing negative commands: Don't bother your brother! Don't scream! Don't forget to do your homework! The negative *tu* command forms of all verbs are formed by the infinitive of the verb preceded by non: *Non andare! Non fare*!

The negative *voi* command forms of all verbs are formed simply by placing *non* before the affirmative *voi* form: *Non credete! Non finite*!

Let's! Let's Not!

The imperative tense is used in other ways as well. For instance, in order to express the idea of "let's . . . ," the imperative of *noi* is used (that would make sense, if you consider that "let's" is the contraction for "let us"). Fortunately, the imperative form of *noi* is identical to its present-indicative form, except that an exclamation mark is used for the imperative. For the negative "let's not," simply place *non* before the verb. Some examples appear in the table below.

▶ **Imperatives in the *Noi* Form**

Infinitive	Present-Indicative Form of Noi	Imperative Form of Noi	Negative Command
andare	andiamo	Andiamo!	Non andiamo!
	(we go)	(Let's go!)	(Let's not go!)
credere	crediamo	Crediamo!	Non crediamo!
	(we believe)	(Let's believe!)	(Let's not believe!)
dormire	dormiamo	Dormiamo!	Non dormiamo!
	(we sleep)	(Let's sleep!)	(Let's not sleep!)
stare	stiamo	Stiamo!	Non stiamo!
	(we stay)	(Let's stay!)	(Let's not stay!)

Who Are You Talking to? Formal and Informal

Need to tell your teacher, supervisor, or the Italian prime minister to do something? Use the subjunctive form of the verb to form the formal commands.

Below are some examples of formal commands.

▶ Formal Commands

Infinitive	Lei	Loro
cantare	Canti!	Cantino!
dormire	Dorma!	Dormano!
finire	Finisca!	Finiscano!
vendere	Venda!	Vendano!

If you remember, some of the verbs have irregular stem changes in the *io* form. Sometimes, this form is used to construct the imperatives of *Lei* and *Loro*.

▶ Formal Commands: Verbs with Stem Changes

Infinitive	Present-Indicative Form of –Io	Imperative Form of –Lei	Imperative Form of Loro
andare (to walk)	vado	Vada!	Vadano!
apparire (to appear)	appaio	Appaia!	Appaiano!
bere (to drink)	bevo	Beva!	Bevano!
cogliere (to pick, to pluck)	colgo	Colga!	Colgano!
dire (to say, to tell)	dico	Dica!	Dicano!
fare (to make)	faccio	Faccia!	Facciano!
porre (to place, to put down)	pongo	Ponga!	Pongano!
rimanere (to stay, to remain)	rimango	Rimanga!	Rimangano!
salire (to climb)	salgo	Salga!	Salgano!
scegliere (to choose, to pick)	scelgo	Scelga!	Scelgano!
sedere (to sit down)	siedo	Sieda!	Siedano!
suonare (to play an instrument)	suono	Suoni!	Suonino!
tradurre (to translate)	traduco	Traduca!	Traducano!
trarre (to draw, to pull)	traggo	Tragga!	Traggano!
udire (to listen)	odo	Oda!	Odano!
uscire (to exit)	esco	Esca!	Escano!
venire (to come)	vengo	Venga!	Vengano!

Finally, some verbs have irregular formal command forms that are not based on any present-indicative forms, and which you will have to memorize. These verbs are listed in the following table.

▶ **Formal Commands: Irregular Verbs**

Infinitive	Lei	Loro
avere	Abbia!	Abbiano!
dare	Dia!	Diano!
essere	Sia!	Siano!
sapere	Sappia!	Sappiano!
stare	Stia!	Stiano

*Note that the same form of the verb is used for the negative formal commands.

Questions

When is *il Colosseo* open? What ingredients are in *ribollito*? Where is *la stazione centrale*? Why is it called *olio extra vergine di oliva*? How much do those Ferragamo shoes cost? Who painted the frescos in the Sistine Chapel? If you want the answers, you'll need to know how to ask the questions!

Interrogatives are words used to form questions. One of the easiest ways to *fare una domanda* (ask a question) in Italian is to place a question mark at the end of a statement. When speaking, the intonation of the voice rises at the end of the sentence. For example:

- Il treno è arrivato. (The train has arrived.)
- Il treno è arrivato? (Has the train arrived?)
- È arrivato il treno. (The train has arrived.)
- È arrivato il treno? (Has the train arrived?)

In questions beginning with an interrogative word, the subject is usually placed at the end of the sentence or after the verb:

- Dove sta Luigi? (Where is Luigi?)
- Quando usciamo? (When do we go out?)

Furthermore, adding the words or phrases *no?*, *non è vero?*, *è vero?*, or *vero?* to the end of a statement will change it into a question:

- Il tuo fratello ha avuto un incidente, non è vero? (Your brother had an accident, didn't he?)
- Sono i padroni, vero? (They are the owners, right?)

Interrogative Adjectives

Interrogative adjectives indicate a quality or indefinite quantity and come with specific nouns. The most common forms are *che* (what? what kind of?), *quale* (which?), and *quanto* (how much? how many?). For example:

- Quali parole ricordi? (Which words do you remember?)
- Che libri leggete? (What books do you read?)
- Quante ragazze vengono? (How many girls are coming?)
- Che ora è? (What time is it?)
- Quanto pane vuoi? (How much bread do you want?)

Notice the difference in meaning between *che* and *quale*. The question *Quali film hai visto?* asks "Which films have you seen?" (For example, *Il postino*, *Ciao professore!* or *La vita è bella*.) The question *Che film hai visto*? asks "What types of films have you seen?" (For example, comedy, romance, or thriller.)

The interrogative adjective *quanto* (how many, how much) agrees in number and gender with the noun it modifies and has four forms (you can see this in the next table).

▶ **Four Forms of *Quanto*? (How Much?/How Many?)**

Gender/ Number	Adjective	Example	English
masculine/ singular	quanto	Quanto tempo fa?	(How long ago?)
masculine/ plural	quanti	Quanti anni hai?	(How old are you?)
feminine/ singular	quanta	Quanta farina c'è?	(How much flour is there?)
feminine/ plural	quante	Quante student- esse ci sono?	(How many stu- dents are there?)

More Questions

Sometimes interrogatives replace nouns altogether, and act as interrogative pronouns that introduce a question. They are:

▶ **Interrogative Pronouns**

Italian	English	Example
Chi?	(Who? Whom?)	Chi sei?
Che/Che cosa/Cosa?	(What?)	Cosa dici?
Quale?	(Which (one/s)?)	Quale giornali vuoi?

Chi is invariable and used exclusively when refer-ring to people: *Chi ha parlato? Di chi stai ridendo?* The gender of the pronoun *chi* is usually recognized in context or by the agreement of the adjective or participle. *Chi hai salutato per prima/primo?*

Che or *che* cosa refers only to a thing and has the significance of *quale/i cose? Che (che cosa) vuoi? Che cosa desideri di più dalla vita?*

Che often appears in the interrogative phrase *che cosa* (what/which thing), though sometimes one of these two words may be dropped. The following three phrases are all equally correct:

- Che cosa bevi? (What are you drinking?)
- Che dici? (What are you saying?)
- Cosa fanno i bambini? (What are the children doing?)

Quale is used to indicate people, animals, or things. It expresses "What is . . . ?" when the answer involves a choice, or when one requests information such as a name, telephone number, or address. *Quale* is invariable in gender. For example: *Quale di voi ha studiato a Parigi? Quale vuoi conservare di queste due fotografie?*

Interrogative Prepositions—Never at the End!

In Italian, a question never ends with a preposition. Prepositions such as *a, di, con,* and *per* always precede the interrogative *chi* (who).

- A chi scrivi? (To whom are you writing?)
- Di chi sono queste chiavi? (Whose keys are these?)
- Con chi escono stasera? (Who[m] are they going out with tonight?)

Useful Question Words

One other group of words is also used in the formation of questions—the interrogative adverbs *come?* (how), *dove?* (where), *perché?* (why), and *quando?* (when).

▶ Interrogative Adverbs

Italian (pronunciation)	English	Example
Come (KOH-meh)?	How?	Come sta Giancarlo?
Dove (DOH-vay)?	Where?	Dov'è la biblioteca?
Perché (pair-KEH)?	Why?	Perché non dormono?
Quando (KWAN-doh)?	When?	Quando parte Pietro?

The following interrogative words are the most commonly used to introduce a question:

A che ora?	At what time?
Come?	How?
Come mai?	How come? Why (on earth)? Why ever?
Dove?	Where?
Perché?	Why?
Quando?	When?
Quanto?	How much?

Two common contractions are *com'è?* (a contraction of *come è?* meaning "how is?") and *dov'è?* (a contraction of *dove è?* meaning "where is?"). Again, note that in Italian the subject and verb are inverted in interrogative sentences:

■ A che ora partono i tuoi amici? (When are your friends leaving?)

■ Come sta Luigi? (How is Louis?)

- Dove sono i bambini? (Where are the children?)
- Dov'è il bambino? (Where is the child?)
- Perché fumi tanto? (Why do you smoke so much?)
- Quanto fa due più tre? (How much is two plus three?)

The subject and verb are not inverted with *come mai*:

- Come mai Umberto non è qui? (How come Umberto is not here?/Why ever isn't Umberto here?)

Pronouns

"I," "you," "he," "she," "we," "they." These are what grammarians call the subject pronouns—they stand in for the subject: "she" instead of "Teresa," or "they" instead of "the children." Observe the following examples in Italian:

- Noi non facciamo così! (We don't do it like that.)
- Domani io farò un esame. (Tomorrow I'm taking an exam.)
- Voi studiate per l'esame? (Are you studying for the exam?)
- Domani vieni a lezione tu? (Tomorrow are you going to the lesson?)

Oftentimes, the subject pronouns are implied in Italian since the form of the verb already indicates the number, gender, and case of the subject. The same sentences in the previous list have the same meaning even with the subject pronouns omitted.

Points of Requirement

There are a few cases in which subject pronouns are required in Italian.

- For contrast: Noi lavoriamo e tu ti diverti. (We work and you amuse yourself.)
- For emphasis: Lo pago io. (I'll pay for it.)
- After the words almeno, anche, magari, neanche, nemmeno, neppure: Neanche noi andiamo al cinema. (We aren't going to the cinema either.)
- When the subject pronoun stands by itself: Chi vuole giocare? Io! (Who wants to play? I do!)

Direct Objects

Remember transitive verbs? They take direct objects, which may be direct object pronouns (*i pronomi diretti*). These pronouns are the person or thing affected by the action of the transitive verb and answer the question "what?" or "whom?" For example:

- She invites the girls. Whom does she invite? The girls.
- I read the book. What do I read? The book.

The nouns "girls" and "book" are direct objects. Direct object pronouns replace direct object nouns:

- She invites the girls. She invites them.
- I read the book. I read it.

The forms of Italian direct object pronouns appear in the following table.

▶ Direct Object Pronouns

Person	Singular	Plural
I	mi (me)	ci (us)
II	ti (you, informal)	vi (you, informal)
III	lo, la (him, her, it)	li, le (them, masculine/feminine)
III	La (you, formal)	Li, Le (you, formal, masculine/feminine)

In Italian, a direct object pronoun is placed immediately before a conjugated verb:

- Se vediamo i ragazzi, li invitiamo. (If we see the boys, we'll invite them.)
- Compra la frutta e la mangia. (He buys the fruit and eats it.)

The only exception to this is when a sentence contains an infinitive. In this case, the object pronoun is attached to the end of it (note that the final −e of the infinitive is dropped):

- È importante mangiarla ogni giorno. (It is important to eat it every day.)
- È una buon'idea invitarli. (It's a good idea to invite them.)

In a negative sentence, the word *non* must come before the object pronoun:

- Non la mangiano. (They don't eat it.)
- Perché non li inviti? (Why don't you invite them?)

It is possible (but not necessary) to omit singular direct object pronouns in front of verbs that begin with a vowel or forms of *avere* that begin with an *h*. However, the plural forms *li* and *le* are never omitted:

- M'ama, non m'ama. [Mi ama, non mi ama.] (He loves me, he loves me not.)
- Il passaporto? Loro non l'hanno [lo hanno]. (The passport? They don't have it.)

A few Italian verbs that take a direct object, such as *ascoltare*, *aspettare*, *cercare*, and *guardare*, correspond to English verbs that are used with prepositions (to listen to, to wait for, to look for, to look at). Compare the following:

- Chi cerchi? (Who are you looking for?)
- Cerco il mio ragazzo. (I'm looking for my boyfriend.)
- Lo cerco già da mezz'ora! (I've been looking for him for half an hour!)

Object pronouns are attached to *ecco* (here) to express the phrases "here I am," "here you are," "here he is," and so on:

- Dov'è la signorina? Eccola! (Where is the young woman? Here she is!)
- Hai trovato le chiavi? Sì, eccole! (Have you found the keys? Yes, here they are!)

Indirect Object Pronouns

Indirect object nouns and pronouns (*i pronomi indiretti*) answer the question "to whom?" or "for whom?" In English, the word "to" is sometimes omitted:

- We gave a cookbook to Uncle John.
- We gave Uncle John a cookbook.

In Italian, the preposition *a* is always used before an indirect object noun:

- Ho regalato un libro di cucina allo zio Giovanni. (I gave a cookbook to Uncle John.)
- Perché non regali un profumo alla mamma? (Why don't you give Mother some perfume?)
- Puoi spiegare questa ricetta a Paolo? (Can you explain this recipe to Paul?)

Indirect object pronouns replace indirect object nouns. They are identical in form to direct object pronouns, except for the third-person forms *gli*, *le*, and *loro*. For all the forms, see the following table.

▶ Indirect Object Pronouns

Person	Singular	Plural
I	mi (to/for me)	ci (to/for us)
II	ti (to/for you, informal)	vi (to/for you, informal)
III	gli, le (to, for him/her)	loro (to/for them)
III	Le (to/for you, formal)	Loro (to/for you, formal)

All indirect object pronouns except *loro* and *Loro* precede a conjugated verb, just like the direct object pronouns (*loro* and *Loro* follow the verb):

- Le ho dato tre ricette. (I gave her three recipes.)
- Ci offrono un caffè. (They offer us a cup of coffee.)
- Parliamo loro domani. (We'll talk to them tomorrow.)

Similarly, indirect object pronouns attach to infinitives, which lose their final –*e*:

■ Non ho tempo di parlargli. (I have no time to talk to him.)

If the infinitive is preceded by a conjugated form of *dovere*, *potere*, or *volere*, the indirect object pronoun may also precede the conjugated verb:

■ Voglio parlargli./Gli voglio parlare. (I want to talk to him.)

Also note that *le* and *gli* are never omitted before a verb beginning with a vowel or an *h*:

■ Le offro un caffè. (I offer her a cup of coffee.)
■ Gli hanno detto "Ciao!" (They said "Ciao!" to him.)

Here are a few common Italian verbs that are often used with indirect object nouns or pronouns. Try to memorize these!

▶ Verbs that Take on Indirect Objects

Italian	English
dare	to give
dire	to say
domandare	to ask
(im)prestare	to lend
insegnare	to teach
mandare	to send
mostrare	to show
offrire	to offer

Italian	English
portare	to bring
preparare	to prepare
regalare	to give (as a gift)
rendere	to return, give back
riportare	to bring back
scrivere	to write
telefonare	to telephone

The Importance of Ne

In Italian, the pronoun *ne* can mean "about," "any," "some," "of it," "of them," from it," "from them," or "from there." It can also replace a prepositional phrase beginning with *da* or *di*. Here are a few examples:

- Parliamo di Mario. (We talk about Mario.)
- Ne parliamo. (We talk about him.)
- Hai bisogno di due francobolli. (You need two stamps.)
- Ne hai bisogno di tre. (You need two of them.)
- Avete molti amici. (You have many friends.)
- Ne avete molti amici. (You have many of them.)
- Ho due fratelli. (I have two brothers.)
- Ne ho due. (I have two of them.)

Combining Direct and Indirect Pronouns

There are many times when the same verb has both a direct object pronoun and an indirect object pronoun. Usually, the indirect object pronoun precedes the direct object pronoun and the indirect object pronouns *mi, ti, ci,* and *vi* change to *me, te, ce,* and *ve*:

■ Renato porta il libro a me. (Renato brings the book to me.)

■ Renato me lo porta. (Renato brings it to me.)

■ Il professore insegna la lezione a voi. (The professor teaches the lesson to you.)

■ Il professore ve l'insegna. (The professor teaches you the lesson.)

For a complete chart of all the double object pronouns, see the following table. Note the economy in words: *gli*, *le*, and *Le* become *glie–* before direct object pronouns and before *ne*, and combine with them to become one word.

▶ **Double Object Pronouns**

Indirect Object	*Lo*	*La*	*Li*	*Le*	*Ne*
mi	me lo	me la	me li	me le	me ne
ti	te lo	te la	te li	te le	te ne
gli, le, Le	glielo	gliela	glieli	gliele	gliene
ci	ce lo	ce la	ce li	ce le	ce ne
vi	ve lo	ve la	ve li	ve le	ve ne
. . . loro	lo . . . loro	la . . . loro	li . . . loro	le . . . loro	ne . . . loro

05 / Getting Around and Being Yourself, Wherever You Are!

I would have gone to Italy, but . . . I should have bought that ticket, but . . . Whether by train, plane, boat, or car, get yourself to Italy. There won't be any excuses after you learn these vocabulary words and the conditional tenses (which were used in the first two sentences of this paragraph).

Coming and Going

Whether you're coming or going, you'll have to make sure your *passaporto* (passport) and *visto* (visa) are in order. Although most border officials do speak English, it wouldn't hurt for you to start practicing your Italian as soon as you get to the border. Take a look at some of the terms you should know.

▶ **At the Border: Common Phrases**

Italian	English
Quando arriviamo alla frontiera?	When do we get to the border?
Ecco il passaporto.	Here's my passport.
Mi fermo una settimana.	I'll be staying a week.

▶ *Italian*   *English*

Italian	English
Sono qui per affari.	I'm here on business.
Sono qui come turista.	I'm here as a tourist (on vacation).
Sono in visita dai miei nonni.	I'm visiting my grandparents.
Posso telefonare al mio consolato?	Can I phone my consulate?
Devo riempire il modulo?	Do I have to fill in this form?

▶ At the Border: Vocabulary

English   *Italian*

English	Italian
color of eyes	il colore degli occhi
color of hair	il colore dei capelli
customs	la dogana
date of birth	la data di nascita
departure	la partenza
divorced	divorziato (male), divorziata (female)
entry visa	il visto d'entrata
exit visa	il visto d'uscita
to extend	prolungare
first name	il nome di battesimo
height	la statura
identity card	la carta d'identità
last name	il cognome
maiden name	il nome da nubile
marital status	lo stato di famiglia
married	sposato (male), sposata (female)
nationality	la nazionalità
occupation	la professione
place of birth	il luogo di nascita
place of residence	la residenza
to renew	rinnovare
signature	la firma
single	celibe (male), nubile (female)

Exchanging money when traveling in Italy doesn't have to be complicated. Often the best rates are through your debit card or credit card using an ATM—check you financial institution before leaving home! Be aware that you'll no longer use lire in Italy. As part of the European Union, Italy now uses the common currency called the Euro.

Passport and Itineraries, You're on Your Way!

You've conjugated verbs, learned to roll your rrrs, can pronounce double consonants, and know the difference between *passato prossimo* and *il futuro*. Now you want to practice your Italian in Italy! Before you go, here is practical information about traveling, including survival phrases, embassy and consulate information, and tour suggestions. *Buon viaggio!*

Get Your Papers in Order

Before your first taste of authentic *crostini misti* and a glass of *Chianti*, you'll have some paperwork to do. Check to see if you need a passport to enter Italy and return home (returning to the United States with an expired passport is illegal).

Visas are generally required for citizens of the United States only if they stay in Italy for longer than three months. If that's the case, you'll need an application form, a detailed itinerary, proof of adequate medical insurance, a valid return airline ticket, and proof of accommodations. Also carry two or more forms of identification on your person, including at least one photo ID. Many banks require several IDs in order to cash traveler's checks.

Getting Through Customs

Going through *la dogana* (customs) shouldn't be much of a bother as long as you have all the right identification. In addition, if you've purchased goods and gifts at a duty-free shop, you'll have to pay a duty on the value of those articles that exceeds the allowance established by the Italian customs service.

If you're an EU citizen you can take the EZ-Pass lanes at the airport and breeze right through customs. It's all part of the efforts to ease border-patrol regulations and ease travel between participating countries.

"Duty-free" simply means that you don't have to pay a tax in the country of purchase. Be sure to keep receipts for major purchases while in Italy—non-EU (European Union) citizens can claim a refund for the value added tax (VAT or IVA).

What if You Lose It?

Sometimes it happens no matter what you do to prevent it. You thought your wallet was safe in your pocket but you misplaced it. Or, your passport fell out of your pocket on that rough ride from Naples to the island of Capri. If you lose your passport, immediately notify the local police and the nearest embassy or consulate. There are consulates in most major Italian cities including Florence, Milan, Naples, Palermo, and Venice. They answer the phone around the clock and also have lists of English-speaking doctors and lawyers.

The U.S. Embassy and Consulate is at Via V. Veneto, 119a, 00187 Rome. They issue new passports the same day but are closed on U.S. and Italian holidays!

Making a Telephone Call

At some point you'll want to speak on the telephone, either to make hotel reservations, purchase tickets to a show, or arrange for a taxi to pick you up. The *alfabeti telefonici* (phonetic alphabet) is useful when spelling out words over the telephone, for example, or when speaking to officials.

Italians tend to use the names of Italian cities (when there is a corresponding town) rather than proper nouns to spell out words. For example, while you might say "M as in Michael," an Italian is more likely to say *M come Milano* (M as in Milan). The following table will give you examples for all other letters, including those five foreign letters that sometimes appear in Italian.

▶ **The Telephone Alphabet:** *A Come Ancona*

Letter	Representative City	Letter	Representative City
A	Ancona	N	Napoli
B	Bologna	O	Otranto
C	Como	P	Padova
D	Domodossola	Q	quarto
E	Empoli	R	Roma
F	Firenze	S	Savona
G	Genova	T	Torino
H	hotel	U	Udine
I	Imola	V	Venezia
J	Jérusalem	W	Washington
K	kilogramma	X	Xeres
L	Livorno	Y	York
M	Milano	Z	Zara

Telephones aren't the only way to communicate in Italy. Internet cafés, Internet bars, and even Internet laundromats are popping up everywhere, so you can access Web-based e-mail providers and even surf the Web while in Italy.

The Government in Italy

Sometimes it seems as though the Italian government strives to reach new levels of dysfunctionality. After all, there have been over sixty governments since the country formed a democratic republic in 1946 following World War II, and political scandals seem to be the norm rather than the exception. On the other hand, it may be that term limits are simply a theoretical concept, and politicians and their parties mutate as the economy, geopolitics, and social programs demand.

Much like many democratic governments today, the Italian government is divided into three branches. The executive branch has two members: the *presidente*, who is elected by an electoral college, and the *primo minis-tero*, who is generally the leader of the party that has the largest representation in the Chamber of Deputies (the prime minister is also sometimes called *il Presidente del Consiglio dei Ministri*). The legislative branch consists of a bicameral *Parlamento*, which includes the *Senato della Repubblica* and the *Camera dei Deputati* (Chamber of Deputies). The *Corte Costituzionale* (Constitutional Court) rounds out the government. For a more in-depth look at Italian government, visit the official Italian government Web site at *www.governo.it*.

Planes, Trains, and Boats

You can practice your Italian even before arriving in Italy if you fly on Alitalia, the Italian national airline. Its planes have a green, white, and red color scheme and the crew wears uniforms designed by—who else?—Italian

designers. Many other airlines have several daily sched-
uled flights into the country from worldwide destinations.
Ready to get on the airplane? The following table has
some useful vocabulary for your airplane trip.

▶ **Vocabulary: On the Plane**

English	Italian
aircraft	l'aereo
land	atterrare
airline	la compagnia aerea
landing	l'atterraggio
approach	avvicinarsi
pilot	il pilota
arrival	l'arrivo
reservation	la prenotazione
crew	l'equipaggio
return flight	il volo di ritorno
destination	la destinazione
seat belt	la cintura di sicurezza
emergency exit	l'uscita d'emergenza
stopover	lo scalo
flight	il volo
takeoff	il decollo
flight attendant	l'assistente di volo
ticket	il biglietto
helicopter	l'elicottero
wing	l'ala

Or Take the Train

Rail travel in Italy is relatively easy, and most cities
and towns have rail service. There are several different
levels of trains on the *Ferrovie dello Stato* or *FS* (Italian

State Railway). Avoid the *locale*, which stops at every station along a line—it's only slightly more expensive to ride the *diretto* or *espresso*, which stops only at major stations. Then there's the *rapido*, or InterCity (IC) train, which travels only to the largest cities. The Eurostar trains are the fast trains, which can be pricey but cut down on travel time considerably.

To find out what *la biglietteria* is and how to inquire about the departure, as well as for other useful vocabulary, take a look at the table below.

▶ **Vocabulary: By Train**

English	Italian
arrival/departure	arrivi/partenze
change trains	cambiar treno
connection	la coincidenza
couchette sleeper	la carrozza cuccette
dining car	il vagone ristorante
express train	il direttissimo
fast train	il diretto
first-aid station	il pronto soccorso
information office	le informazioni
long distance express	il rapido
money exchange	il cambio
motorail service	la littorina
platform	il binario
rail car	l'automotrice
restaurant	il ristorante
restroom	il gabinetto
sleeper/sleeping car	il vagone letto
suburban train	il treno suburbano
ticket window	la biglietteria
timetable	l'orario
waiting room	la sala d'aspetto

Amenities?

Not all Italian hotels have air conditioning, for example. So, sorry to break it to you but you'll just have to get used to it! And in the economy *pensioni* and *alberghi*, you'll probably have to walk down the hall to use the bathroom. But then, you're here to see the ancient ruins, the Donatello sculptures, and the *affreschi* (frescoes) by Ghirlandio, not to watch TV in your hotel room. For some help in how to check in and other related vocabulary, see the following table.

▶ **Vocabulary: Checking In**

English	Italian
bath	il bagno
bill	il conto
blanket	la coperta
concierge	il portinaio
corridor	il corridoio
drapery	la tenda
elevator	l'ascensore
heating	il riscaldamento
lamp	la lampada
lobby	l'atrio
mattress	il materasso
mirror	lo specchio
pillow	il cuscino
plug	la spina
refrigerator	il frigorifero
room	la camera
shower	la doccia
sink	il lavandino
terrace	il terrazzo
towel	l'asciugamano

In big tourist towns and at expensive hotels the staff almost always speaks at least enough English to help those who haven't yet mastered Italian. Still, trying to speak Italian will definitely ingratiate you in the eyes of the staff—and it might even get you a better room.

Conditional Use

The present-conditional tense (*condizionale presente*) is equivalent to the English constructions of "would" + verb (for example: I would never forget). Forming conditionals is easy: Just take any verb, drop the final –*e* in its infinitive form, and add an appropriate ending—endings are the same for all three conjugation groups of verbs. The only spelling change occurs with –*are* verbs, which change the *a* of the infinitive ending to *e*. You will need to be familiar with this tense if you want to be polite when traveling in Italy.

▶ **Conjugating Verbs in the Present Conditional**

Pronoun	–are (Parlare)	–ere (Credere)	–ire (Sentire)
io	parlerei	crederei	sentirei
tu	parleresti	crederesti	sentiresti
lui, lei, Lei	parlerebbe	crederebbe	sentirebbe
noi	parleremmo	crederemmo	sentiremmo
voi	parlereste	credereste	sentireste
loro, Loro	parlerebbero	crederebbero	sentirebbero

Reflexive verbs follow the same scheme, with the addition of the reflexive pronouns *mi, ti, si, ci, vi,* or *si* when conjugating them: *mi laverei, ti laveresti, si laverebbe, ci laveremmo, vi lavereste, si laverebbero.* Here are some examples of conditional-tense sentences:

■ Vorrei un caffè. (I would like a coffee.)

- Scriverei a mia madre, ma non ho tempo. (I would write to my mother, but I don't have time.)
- Mi daresti il biglietto per la partita? (Would you give me a ticket for the game?)

We Could Have...

But at the stroke of midnight my coach turns into a *zucca*! The conditional perfect (*condizionale passato*), like all compound tenses in Italian, is formed with the *condizionale presente* of the auxiliary verb *avere* or *essere* and the past participle of the acting verb. Conjugated forms of *avere* and *essere* appear here.

▶ *Condizionale Presente* **of the Verbs** *Avere* **and** *Essere*

Person	Singular	Plural
I	(io) avrei, sarei	(noi) avremmo, saremmo
II	(tu) avresti, saresti	(voi) avreste, sareste
III	(lui, lei, Lei) avrebbe, sarebbe	(loro, Loro) avrebbero, sarebbero

Here are a few examples of the *condizionale passato* in action. Remember that verbs conjugated with *essere* must change their endings to agree in number and gender with the subject:

- Avremmo potuto ballare tutta la notte. (We could have danced all night.)
- Avreste dovuto invitarlo. (You ought to have invited him.)
- Saremmo andati volentieri alla Scala, ma non abbiamo potuto. (We would gladly have gone to La Scala, but we weren't able to.)
- Mirella sarebbe andata volentieri al cinema. (Mirella would have been happy to go to the cinema.)

Sightseeing Tips and Terms

On your mark, get set, sightsee! It's tempting to try to see everything that's in the guidebooks, checking off churches and museums and historical monuments like a grocery list. Here's a tip: Do as the Italians do and slow down. Enjoy a walk down the street, chat up a store clerk, listen to schoolchildren singing.

The real Italy isn't in a tour or a book or a museum—it's experienced during a delicious lunch in a small, out-of-the-way trattoria, in a park with the smell of cyprus trees everywhere, or in the sound of the church bells every hour. After all, this is the country of *la dolce vita*. For your own *giro turistico* (sightseeing tour), check out this vocabulary table.

▶ **Vocabulary: Sightseeing**

English	Italian
district	il quartiere
embassy	l'ambasciata
excavations	gli scavi
farmhouse	la cascina
fountain	la fontana
gallery	la galleria
gate	il portone
landscape	il paesaggio
memorial	il monumento commemorativo
mountain	la montagna
museum	il museo
old town	il centro storico
palace	il palazzo
park	il parco
port	il porto
river	il fiume
subway	la metropolitana

English	Italian
taxi	il tassì
valley	la valle
waterfall	la cascata

Travel by Water

Italy is a peninsula with beaches that encircle most of the country and has a rich maritime history. There are the islands of Capri and Ischia off of Naples, and the Aeolian Islands where volcanoes still spew lava. There are the islands of Sicilia and Sardegna (or Sardinia), homes to two very different cultures, yet still part of Italy. Then there's *La Serenissima* (the Most Serene One), otherwise known as Venezia, the city on the sea, with lagoons instead of streets and narrow, twisting walkways. (Venezia is accessible primarily by *vaporetto*, water taxi, or *gondola*. The city itself is comprised of 118 bodies of land in a lagoon, connected to the mainland by a thin causeway.)

For some maritime vocabulary, navigate your way to the next table.

▶ Vocabulary: On Board

English	Italian
anchor	l'ancora
barge	la scialuppa
bay	la baia
boat	la barca
bow	la prua
captain	il capitano
deck	la coperta
ferry	il traghetto
fishing trawler	la barca da pesca
gangway	la passerella

English	Italian
lifeboat	la scialuppa di salvataggio
lighthouse	il faro
mast	l'albero
motorboat	il motoscafo
pier	il pontile
rudder	il timone
sailboat	la barca a vela
steamer	il vaporetto

Museums, Theatre, and Art

Whether you travel to Italy, page through a coffee-table book featuring Italian artists, or listen to opera on the radio, the plethora of Italian art is unavoidable.

A wide variety of amazing artwork has been created in Italy from before the Roman Empire up to the present day, and it provides a unique way to study the language while learning more about the artistic patrimony of Italy.

The Big Names

Michelangelo, Raffaello, Leonardo, and Donatello have at least one thing in common: Most people nowadays know these artists by their first names. Obviously, they had *cognomi* (last names) too:

- Michelangelo Buonarroti
- Raffaello Sanzio
- Donato di Betto Bardi (Donatello)
- Leonardo da Vinci

Along the Way, Keep in Mind

When referring to a particular artistic period in a century between 1100 and 1900, Italians drop the *mille* (thousand). For example, they call the 1300s *il Trecento,* the 1400s *il Quattrocento,* and so on.

Also, you should know that there's a price to pay for everything—even church. So be aware! Some churches in Italy now request an entrance fee to offset the cost of maintenance, claiming that the artwork found on their walls, by such artists as Filippo Brunelleschi, Masaccio, and Giotto, are equal to any found in museums. Town residents are exempt from paying though.

Art in Other Forms

Marble, wood, bronze. If it was solid and durable, chances are an artist would grab a chisel and begin to sculpt. Donatello, for example, was an extremely influential Florentine sculptor of the *Quattrocento.* He did freestanding sculptures in marble, bronze, and wood, and was also known for a new way of doing shallow relief that gave a sense of depth through using perspective rather than through the use of high relief. Michelangelo believed it was his duty to liberate the figure that was straining to be released from the marble. His slave series, several of which can be viewed in Florence's *Galleria dell'Accademia,* are perhaps the best examples of how he chipped away just enough marble to liberate the figures.

At the Museum

So do you want to see these great works of art for yourself? If so, check out these top-ten not-to-be-missed Italian museums:

1. Galleria dell'Accademia, Firenze
2. Galleria Borghese, Roma
3. Galleria degli Uffizi, Firenze
4. Museo della Scuola Grande di San Rocco, Venezia

5. Museo di Capodimonte, Napoli
6. Musei Vaticani (a group of several museums housing world-class treasures)
7. Palazzo Farnese, Roma
8. Museo del Risorgimento, Milano
9. Museo Egizio and Galleria Sabauda, Torino
10. Galleria Regionale della Sicilia, Palermo

You're standing on line at the *Uffizi* in Florence or the *Capodimonte Museum* in Naples and can't wait to see all that amazing artwork. Or you're a student in an art history class studying Michelangelo, Ghirlandaio, and Caravaggio. Put your free time to good use and review some vocabulary words that relate to art and museums.

▶ **Vocabulary: At the Museum**

English	Italian
apprentice	l'apprendista
art	l'arte
artist	l'artista
canvas	la tela
caption	la didascalia
corridor	il corridoio
frame	la cornice
gallery	la galleria
marble	il marmo
masterpiece	il capolavoro
paint, to	dipingere
paint	la vernice
paintbrush	il pennello
painter	il pittore
relief	il rilievo
Renaissance	il Rinascimento
sculpt	scolpire

English	Italian
sculptor	il scultore
sculpture	la scultura
studio	la bottega

Theatre or L'Opera

There might not be another pastime in Italy that is more closely associated with the Italian language than opera. The theatrical form, combining acting, singing, and classical music, originated in Italy more than 400 years ago. Most operas were originally sung in Italian, and today there are historic opera houses throughout Italy where the divas still sing.

The common operatic term *bel canto* (beautiful singing) points out why so many people refer to Italian as a language that's "sung" by native speakers. Since Italian speakers place the vowels in a forward position (in front of the mouth) just as singers do when singing, it's easy for Italians to switch from speaking to singing. That's probably why so many Italians seem to be blessed with "natural" singing voices. The formation of vowels is integral not only in singing opera but in speaking Italian as well.

If you want to get a head start on understanding a performance, be sure to read the *libretto* (literally, "little book") first. The *libretto* is a play-by-play of all the action onstage, and reading it will enhance your time at the theater. Although you might not be able to follow the songs word for word, what's more important is to get a feel for the action, the excitement, and the drama.

Here are just a few operas that are recognized as masterpieces and are sure to give you a thrill:

- *Aida*, by Giuseppi Verdi, was first produced in Cairo in 1871. The opera is set in ancient Egypt and is named after the Ethiopian princess who is its heroine.
- *Il Barbiere di Siviglia* (*The Barber of Seville*) is a comic opera composed by Gioacchino Rossini and first produced in Rome in 1816. The barber of the title is Figaro, a character who also appears in Mozart's *Le Nozze di Figaro*, a sequel.
- *La Bohème* is an opera in four acts by Giacomo Puccini, first produced in Turin in 1896.
- *Rigoletto* is an opera by Verdi produced in Venice in 1851. The title is taken from its baritone hero, a tragic court jester. "La donna è mobile" (the woman is fickle) is its most famous aria.
- *La Traviata* is another opera written by Verdi. The title is variously interpreted to mean "the fallen woman" or "the woman gone astray." The work, in three acts, was first performed in Venice in 1853.

If you ever have the opportunity, hearing a performance at Milano's *La Scala* will leave you speechless. *Bravissimi!* To help you find your way out there, you might need to know a few vocabulary words.

▶ **Vocabulary: At the Theatre**

English	Italian
act	l'atto
backstage	il retroscena
ballet	il balletto
ballet dancer	il ballerino
cadence	la cadenza
check room	il guardaroba
comedy	la commedia
comic opera	l'opera buffa

English	Italian
concert	il concerto
conductor	il direttore d'orchestra
costumes	i costumi
curtain	il sipario
dance	la danza
duet	il duetto
intermission	l'intervallo
lyric	il lirico
music	la musica
musical	il musicale
overture	il preludio
performance	la rappresentazione
play	l'opera drammatica
producer	il produttore
production	la messa in scena
program	il programma
scene	la scena
scenery	lo scenario
show	lo spettacolo
singer	il cantante
song	il canzone
stage	il palcoscenico
symphony	la sinfonia
tenor	il tenore
ticket	il biglietto
voice	la voce

Golden Arches in Italy?

McDonald's might have served billions of hamburgers beneath its neon arches, but it was the Romans who put the *arco in architettura*, using this design element to build aqueducts, stadiums, villas, and palaces. Learning about architecture is another way to increase your Italian vocabulary, whether you'd like to learn about the three primary orders of columns—*corinto, dorico, or ionico*—or the many different types of architectural styles—*bizantino, gotico, romanico, rinascimento, manierismo, barocco.* Another example? The palladium window derives from an Italian architect, Andrea Palladio, who led a revival of classical architecture in sixteenth-century Italy and designed many major buildings, including the church of *San Giorgio Maggiore* in Venice, built in 1566.

If you are interested in learning more about architecture and have some time on your hands, try the ten-volume treatise *De Architectura* written in the first century B.C. by Vitruvius, a Roman architect and military engineer. The work is considered the bible of classical architectural theory and also served to inspire the Italian Renaissance's architects and educated men.

The Bible's Influence on Art

If a priest wanted to teach his congregation about the Bible, and virtually all the common folk were illiterate, how else could he convey his message? With pictures! That's one reason why so many churches in Italy have paintings, frescoes, and mosaics everywhere. Commissioned artists created pictorial representations of Biblical stories, from the flood to the martyrdom of saints, from heaven to hell, from Christ's birth to His crucifixion and resurrection. Since very few people could read, this was one way for them to visualize the sermons offered from the pulpit. Images of sinners burning in Hell probably convinced a number of churchgoers to mind their actions.

It's not surprising to see so many impressive-looking churches in a country where the seat of Roman Catholicism is located. Throughout Italy, there are cathedrals and basilicas in styles such as Byzantine, Gothic, Romanesque, and Renaissance. If you're looking for some of the best examples of celestial art and architecture, you can't go wrong visiting these churches:

- Basilica di San Francesco, Assisi: Built in memorial of St. Francis, this unique church, with two separate levels, has a number of important frescoes by artists such as Giotto, Cimabue, Simone Martini, and Pietro Lorenzetti.
- Cattedrale, Battistero, e Campanile, Pisa: It's not just the Leaning Tower of Pisa! The green-and-white marble stonework of the adjacent buildings is every bit as stunning.
- Duomo e Battistero, Firenze: The octagonal duomo by Filippo Brunelleschi can be seen for miles around, while the ceiling of the Baptistery is covered in amazing mosaics.
- Basilica di San Marco, Venezia: The curving domes of the church are encrusted with golden mosaics that are the epitome of Byzantine art.
- San Miniato al Monte, Firenze: This church overlooking a hillside has many important frescoes.
- Sant'Ambrogio, Milano: This is an amazing Gothic church in the center of the city. Visitors can even walk on the roof for a closeup look at the spires.
- Santa Maria Novella, Firenze: Wealthy businessmen commissioned several of the city's most important Renaissance artists to create frescoes in the chapels that line this church.

Next, get to know some architectural jargon.

▶ Vocabulary: Architecture

English	Italian	English	Italian
abbey	l'abbazia	cloister	il chiostro
altar	l'altare	crucifix	il crocifisso
arch	l'arco	Last Supper	il cenacola
balcony	la loggia	nave	la navata
baptistery	il battistero	palace	il palazzo
bell tower	il campanile	pilaster	il pilastro
canopy	il baldacchino	refectory	il refettorio
chapel	la cappella	rose window	il rosone
church	la chiesa		

Survival Phrases and in Case of an Emergency

As you get to the end of this book, you may not remember the difference between transitive and intransitive verbs, or the indirect object pronouns. However, make sure you commit to memory the following Italian phrases, essential for visitors who would like to ingratiate themselves with native Italians. If you try to communicate in Italian, it's likely they'll return the thoughtfulness with goodwill and graciousness.

- A domani! (See you tomorrow.)
- A presto! (See you soon.)
- Arrivederci! (Good-bye!)
- Buon giorno! (Good morning!)
- Buon pomeriggio! (Good afternoon!)
- Buona sera! (Good evening!)
- Buonanotte! (Good night!)
- Come sta? (How are you?)
- Come va? (How're you doing?)
- Ci sentiamo bene. (We're feeling fine.)
- Ciao! (Hi!/Bye!)

- Come si chiama? (What is your name?)
- Di dov'è? (Where are you from?)
- Piacere di conoscerLa. (Pleased to meet you.)
- Siamo qui da una settimana. (We've been here for a week.)

Just in Case: Emergency Terms

Sometimes it happens. The rental car breaks down, you lose your wallet, or worse. If you find yourself in a situation like this, don't panic, and concentrate on trying to explain what happened to *la polizia* at *la stazione di polizia*.

▶ **Vocabulary: Police Station**

English	Italian	English	Italian
an accident	incidente	judge	il giudice
arrest, to	arrestare	key	la chiave
attorney	l'avvocato	money	i soldi
bag	la borsa	necklace	la collana
billfold	il portafoglio	police	la polizia
briefcase	la cartella	prison	la prigione
court	il tribunale	purse	il borsellino
crime	il delitto	ring	l'anello
custody	la detenzione	suitcase	la valigia
drugs	le droghe	thief	il ladro
guilt	la colpa	verdict	la sentenza
handbag	la borsetta	watch	l'orologio

Appendix A / Italian to English Dictionary

accompagnare	to accompany
acqua	water
adagio	slowly
addome	abdomen
adesso	now
aeroporto	airport
affardellare	to bundle together, to pack
affinché	so that; in order that
affittare	to rent
agganciare	to fasten, to attach
aglio	garlic
agnello	lamb
ahimè	alas
ala	wing
allegria	happiness
allegro	happy
allenare	to train
almeno	at least
altura	hill
ambulanza	ambulance

amore	love
anatra	duck
anche	also
ancora	still, again, yet
andare	to go
anello	ring
anno	year
antefatto	prior event
anteporre	to put before
antipasti	appetizers
anziché	rather than
appartamento	apartment
appartenere	to belong
approvare	to approve, to accept
appunto	exactly
aprire	to open
arachide	peanut
aragosta	lobster
aria	air
armadio	closet
arrivare	to arrive
ascensore	elevator
ascoltare	to listen to
assegno	check
atterrare	to land
attirare	to attract
atto	act
attore	actor
aula	classroom
autostrada	highway
autunno	autumn
azzurro	blue
babbo	father, dad(dy)

baciare	to kiss
bacio	kiss
bagno	bathroom, bath
baia	bay
balocco	toy
bambino	child
bambola	doll
banca	bank
banchiere	banker
banco	counter
barba	beard
barca	boat
basilico	basil
battere	to beat, to hit, to strike
benché	although
bestia	beast
bevanda	drink
bianco	white
Bibbia	Bible
bibita	drink, beverage
biblioteca	library
biglietto	ticket
binario	track, platform
birra	beer
biscotto	cookie, biscuit
bistecca	steak
bloccare	to block, to cut off
bocca	mouth
bollo	stamp
bottega	shop
bottiglia	bottle
bottone	button
braccare	to hunt

braccio	arm
bruno	brown
brutto	ugly
burro	butter
busta	envelope
cadere	to fall
calciare	to kick
calcio	soccer
caldo	heat
calendario	calendar
calmo	calm
camera da letto	bedroom
cameriere	waiter
camminare	to walk
campagna	countryside
canale	channel
cane	dog
cantina	cellar
capitare	to happen
cappello	hat
cappotto	coat
capra	goat
carcere	jail, prison
carta	paper
carta di credito	credit card
cartolina	postcard
cavallo	horse
caverna	cave
celare	to hide, to conceal
cercare	to look for
chiacchiere	to chat
chiaro	clear
chiave	key

chiesa	church
chirurgo	surgeon
cinghiale	wild boar
cinta	belt
cipolla	onion
circo	circus
cittadino	citizen
classe	classroom
clima	climate
cognata	sister-in-law
cognato	brother-in-law
colle	hill
coltello	knife
compleanno	birthday
coniglio	rabbit
conte	count
conto	bill, account
contrarre	to contract
controllare	to check
costume da bagno	bathing suit
cotone	cotton
cravatta	tie
creanza	politeness
crema	cream
cricca	gang
crostaceo	shellfish
cucinare	to cook
cugina	cousin (female)
cugino	cousin (male)
cuoio	leather
curare	to cure
dabbasso	downstairs
dabbene	honest

danno	danger, harm
dappertutto	everywhere
dappoco	worthless
dattero	date
davanti	in front
davanzo	more than enough
davvero	really, truly, indeed
debellare	to defeat
debilitare	to weaken
debole	weak
decantare	to praise
decenne	decade
decollo	take off
deflazione	deflation
deliberare	to deliberate, to discuss
democratico	democratic
denaro	money
dentro	inside
depositare	to deposit
derubare	to rob
deserto	desert
destra	right
deviazione	detour
diario	diary, journal
dibattito	debate, discussion
dieta	diet
dietro	in the back
difetto	defect
dilungare	to lengthen
dio	god
dipingere	to paint
direttiva	directive
distruggere	to destroy

ditto	finger
divano	sofa, couch
dizionario	dictionary
dogana	customs
domani	tomorrow
donna	woman
dono	gift
dopodomani	day after tomorrow
dormire	to sleep
dovunque	everywhere, anywhere
dozzina	dozen
dritta	right hand
dunque	therefore; well (then)
duomo	cathedral
durante	during, throughout
e, ed (before vowels)	and
ebbene	well (then)
eccellere	to excel
eccetto	except
eccezionale	exceptional
economico	inexpensive
edicola	newsstand, bookstall
elementari	primary school
elettrificare	to electrify
elezione	election
eliminare	to eliminate
eludere	to elude, to escape
emergenza	emergency
emotivo	emotional
empire	to fill (up)
encomiare	to commend
enorme	enormous, huge
enoteca	wine bar

entrambi	both
entrante	coming, next
entrare	to fit, to enter
epidemia	epidemic
Epifania	Epiphany (Jan. 6)
epoca	epoch, age, era, time
equatore	equator
equino	horse
ergere	to raise, to lift up
eroe	hero
esatto	exact
esercito	army
esimio	outstanding, distinguished
esito	result
esotico	exotic
esplicito	explicit
est	east
estate	summer
estero	foreign
evadere	to escape, to run away
evasivo	evasive
evento	event
evitare	to avoid
fa	ago
fabbrica	factory
faccenda	thing, matter
facciata	façade
facinoroso	violent
fama	report, fame, rumor
fame	hunger
famiglia	family
famoso	famous; well-known
fanale	light, lamp

fango	mud, mire
fantasma	ghost, phantom
farmacia	pharmacy
farmaco	drug
fascismo	fascism
fautore	supporter
favella	speech
febbre	fever
felce	fern
felino	feline
fermare	to stop
fervente	fervent, fervid, ardent
festa	holiday, festival
fiducia	trust
figlia	daughter
figlio	son
fila	line, row
fine settimana	weekend
finestra	window
finora	so far, up till now
firmare	to sign
fisso	set, fixed
fiume	river
flettere	to bend
fluire	to flow
folla	crowd
forchetta	fork
formaggio	cheese
forte	strong
fragola	strawberry
fratellastro	stepbrother, half brother
fratello	brother
frustrare	to frustrate, to thwart

frutta	fruit
fulmine	lightning
fungo	mushroom
fuoco	fire
fuori	outside
futuro	future
gabinetto	toilet
galera	prison
gamba	leg
gatto	cat
gelare	to freeze
gelato	ice cream
genero	son-in-law
genitori	parents
gente	people
gergale	slang
già	already
giacca	jacket
giacere	to lie
giallo	yellow
giardino	garden
giocare	to play
giorno festivo	holiday
girare	to turn
gironzolare	to stroll about
giungla	jungle
giurare	to swear, to take an oath
giusto	just, right, correct
gonfiare	to inflate, to blow up
gonna	skirt
gradire	to appreciate, to enjoy
grande	big, large
grasso	fat

grattacapo	trouble
gravare	to burden
greve	heavy
grigio	gray
griglia	grill
grullo	silly
guanti	gloves
guardare	to watch
gustare	to taste
ieri	yesterday
igiene	hygiene, health
ignorare	to ignore
ignoto	unknown
illecito	illicit
illegale	illegal
immenso	immense
immigrare	to immigrate
imparare	to learn
impegno	engagement, commitment
imperizia	inexperience
importare	to import
impostare	to mail
imprecare	to curse
imprestare	to lend
improprio	improper
in ritardo	later
inabitable	uninhabitable
incinta	pregnant
incivile	uncivilized, barbaric
incominciare	to start, to begin
incrocio	intersection, crossing
indenne	unharmed, unhurt
indire	to announce, to proclaim

indirizzo	address
indispettire	to irritate, to annoy
indole	nature, temperament
indovinare	to guess
infatti	in fact
infermiere	nurse
infinitivo	infinitive
inflazione	inflation
influsso	influence
ingresso	entrance
iniziare	to begin
insistere	to insist
insolito	unusual, strange, odd
intermezzo	intermission
internazionale	international
intero	entire, whole
inutile	useless, hopeless
invece	instead
inverno	winter
inviare	to send
ironia	irony
isola	island
itinerario	itinerary
labbro	lip
lacrima	tear, drop
ladro	thief
laggiù	down there
lago	lake
lampada	lamp
lampante	clear
lampo	lightning
lampone	raspberry
larghezza	width, breadth

largo	wide
lassù	up there
latte	milk
latteria	dairy store
lattuga	lettuce
lavadino	sink
lavarsi	to wash oneself
lavatrice	washing machine
leale	loyal, sincere
leggere	to read
leggero	light
legno	wood
lenzuolo	sheet
letizia	joy
lettera	letter
letto	bed
levante	east
levare	to raise, to lift up
lezione	lesson
libero	free
libertà	freedom
libreria	bookstore
libro	book
liceo	high school
limitare	to limit
limone	lemon
lingua	language, tongue
litigare	to fight, argue
locale	public place
lontano	far
lotta	struggle
lotteria	lottery
luce	light

luna	moon
luogo	place
macchè	not at all
macchina	engine, machine
maciullare	to crush
madornale	gross
madre	mother
madrelingua	native language
madrina	godmother, sponsor, matron
maestro	teacher, expert
magazzino	store, warehouse, depot
maggioranza	majority
magia	magic
maglione	sweater
magro	thin
maiale	pork, pig
malo	bad, evil, wicked
mancanza	lack, want
mandare	to send
mangiare	to eat
maniera	manner
mantenere	to keep
mare	sea
marito	husband
materasso	mattress
materia	subject
matita	pencil
matrigna	stepmother
mattina	morning
medesimo	same
mediante	by
medico	doctor
meglio	better

meno	less
mente	mind
mento	chin
menzogna	lie
mercato	market
mescolare	to mix
metà	half
mettersi	to put on
mezzanotte	midnight
mezzogiorno	noon
minestra	soup
mischiare	to mix
misurare	to measure
mito	myth
moglie	wife
montagna	mountain
monumento	monument
mostra	exhibit, fair
mostro	monster
motivo	reason, cause, grounds
multa	fine, ticket
muraglia	wall
museo	museum
narrativa	fiction, narrative
nascondere	to hide
naso	nose
Natale	Christmas
natura	nature
nazione	nation
neanche	not even
nebbia	fog, mist
nefando	wicked
negletto	neglected

negozio	store, shop, deal
nemmeno	not even
nero	black
nespola	medlar
neutro	neutral
neve	snow
nevicare	to snow
niente	nothing
ninnolo	toy, plaything
nipote	nephew, niece, grandchild
nitido	neat, clear
nitore	brightness, lucidity
nocciolina	peanut
noce	walnut
nocivo	harmful
nodo	knot, bond, tie
noia	boredom, tedium
noiso	boring
nomina	appointment
non	not
nonna	grandmother
nonno	grandfather
nord	north
notizia	news
noto	well-known
notte	night
novello	new
nozze	wedding, marriage
nube	clouds
nudo	naked, nude, bare
nuora	daughter-in-law
nuotare	to swim
nutrire	to nourish

nuvola	cloud
occhiali	glasses
occidente	west
occorrere	to need
occultare	to hide
oceano	ocean
offendere	to offend, to insult
offrire	to offer
oggetto	object
oggi	today
ogni	every, each
ognuno	everyone, everybody
olfatto	sense of smell
olio	olive
ombra	shade, dark, shadows
onda	wave
onestà	honesty, integrity
onore	honor
operaio	worker
opificio	factory
oppure	else, or
optare	to opt
orario	schedule
orbita	orbit, limits
ordinare	to order
orecchio	ear
orgoglio	pride
orlare	to edge, to border
orrore	horror, disgust
orso	bear
ortaggio	vegetable
orto	garden
ospitale	hospital

ostaggio	hostage
ostello	hostel
osteria	inn
ostruire	to obstruct
ottimo	excellent, best
ove	where
ovest	west
ovino	sheep
ovvio	obvious
pacchetto	package
pace	peace
padre	father
padrino	godfather
padrone	master, owner, proprietor
pagamento	payment
pagare	to pay
pagina	page
palla	ball
palpare	to feel
pancetta	bacon
pane	bread
panificio	bakery
panino	roll
panno	cloth
pantaloni	pants, slacks, trousers
papà	dad, daddy, pop
papa	Pope
paradiso	paradise, heaven
parcheggiare	to park
parecchio	several, quite a few
parente	relative
parere	opinion
parete	wall

partenza	departure
Pasqua	Easter
passaporto	passport
passare	to pass
pasticceria	pastry shop
patata	potato
patrigno	stepfather
pavimento	floor
pecora	sheep
pelle	leather
penisola	peninsula
perdurare	to continue, to last, to go on
pericolo	danger, risk, hazard
pesce	fish
pezzo	piece
pianterreno	ground floor
piattino	saucer
piede	foot
pieno	full
piglio	to look
pillola	pill
pioggia	rain
piovere	to rain
piscina	swimming pool
più	more
piuttosto	rather
poco	not very much
poiché	since
pollo	chicken
polmone	lung
polso	wrist
pomodoro	tomato
ponte	bridge

porta	door
positivo	positive
posteggiare	to park
pozzo	well
predone	robber
preferire	to prefer
pregare	to pray, to beg, to ask
pregno	pregnant
prendere	to take
prezzo	price
prima classe	first class
primavera	spring
primeggiare	to excel
primo ministro	prime minister
principale	main
principianti	beginners
profondo	deep
promettere	to promise
pulire	to clean, to scrub
qua	here
quaderno	notebook
quadrato	square
quadro	painting, picture
quaggiù	down here
qualcuno	someone, somebody
qualora	in case, if
qualsiasi	any
qualunque	any
quando	when
quantità	quantity
quanto	how much
quantunque	although
quartiere	neighborhood

quasi	almost, nearly
quassù	up here
quattrini	money
quattrocchi	face to face
querela	action, suit
questione	issue
questura	police headquarters
qui	here
quietanza	receipt
rabbonire	to calm down, to pacify
raccolta	collection
raccontare	to tell, narrate
raddrizzare	to straighten
ragazza	girl
ragazzo	boy
rallegrare	to cheer up
rapido	quick, fast
rapina	robbery, plunder, booty
rapporto	connection, report
rasare	to shave, to cut, to trim
rasoio	razor
ratto	rat
re	king
realtà	reality
reddito	income, revenue
regalare	to give a gift
reggia	royal palace
regina	queen
regno	kingdom, realm
regola	rule
reintegrare	to restore
rena	sand
rene	kidney

reparto	unit, division, section
reputare	to consider
resa	surrender
respiro	breath
restaurare	to restore
ricchezza	wealth
ricco	rich
ricevuta	receipt, bill
rilassare	to relax
rima	rhyme
rimanere	to remain
ripieno	stuffed, filled
riscaldare	to warm, to heat
ristorante	restaurant
ritmo	rhythm
rito	ritual
rivista	magazine
robusto	stout, strong
rosso	red
rubinetto	faucet
sacerdote	priest
sagra	festival
salario	salary
saldo	balance
salire	to get on, to board
salpare	to sail
salubre	healthy
salutare	to greet
sapone	soap
sborsare	to pay
scala	staircase
scaldarsi	to heat
scarpa	shoe

scatola	box
scegliere	to choose
sciare	to ski
sciopero	strike
scoiattolo	squirrel
scolare	to drain
scorso	last, past
scrostare	to scrape
sebbene	although
secco	dry
secolo	century
segreto	secret
semaforo	traffic light
sentiero	path, footpath
sentito	sincere
senza	without
sera	evening
serpente	snake
sesso	sex
sete	thirst
settentrione	north
sfidare	to challenge
sfortuna	misfortune, bad luck
sforzo	effort
sgabello	stool, footstool
siccome	as
sicurezza	safety
sicuro	safe, sure
signora	Mrs., Ms., woman
signore	Mr., Sir, man
soggetto	subject
soggiorno	living room
soglio	throne, seat

sogno	dream, wishful thinking
solamente	only
sole	sun
soltanto	only, all, just, alone
somigliare	to resemble
sopra	on top
sordo	deaf
sorella	sister
sorellastra	stepsister, half sister
sorridere	to smile
sorriso	smile
sotto	under
spalla	shoulder
specchio	mirror
spesso	often
spettacolo	show
spiegare	to explain
spingere	to push
spolverare	to dust
sporco	dirty
sportello	ticket window
squadra	team
stanza	room
Stati Uniti	United States
stazione	station
strada	street, road
strano	strange
sudore	sweat
suggerire	to suggest
suocera	mother-in-law
suocero	father-in-law
suonare	to ring
sveglia	alarm clock

svendita	sale
tabacco	tobacco
tacchino	turkey
tacito	silent; tacit
taco	heel
tagliare	to cut
tale	such
tappeto	rug, carpet
tariffa	fare
tasca	pocket
tasse	taxes
tavola	table
tazza	cup
teatro	theater
telefono	telephone
tempesta	storm
tentare	to try, to attempt
terra	earth, land, country
testa	head
timido	shy
tomba	tomb, grave
tonaca	habit
torace	chest
tra	between
tragedia	tragedy
tragitto	journey, way, route
tramare	to plot, to scheme
tranne	except for, but
trappola	trap
treno	train
triste	sad, sorrowful
tritare	to chop
troppo	too much, too many

trovare	to find
turbare	to disturb, to trouble
turista	tourist
tuttora	still
ubbidire	to obey
ubriacarsi	to get drunk
ubriaco	drunk
uccello	bird
uccidere	to kill
udibile	audible
udienza	hearing, audience
udire	to hear, to listen to
uditorio	audience
ufficiale	official
uggioso	boring
uguale	(exactly) the same
ultimare	to complete
ultimo	last, final
umanità	humanity
umile	humble, modest
un	a, an, one
una	a, an, one
ungere	to grease, to oil
unificare	to unify
unione	union, uniting
università	university
universo	universe
uno	one, a, an
uomo	man
uova	egg
uragano	hurricane, storm, tempest
urgente	urgent
urlare	to shout

urlo	roar, howl
usato	used
uscire	to go out, to leave
uscita	exit
utile	useful
vacante	vacant
vacanza	vacation
vaglia	money order
valevole	valid
valle	valley
vaniglia	vanilla
vantaggio	advantage
varcare	to cross
vegetale	vegetable
veleno	poison
vento	wind
ventre	stomach
verde	green
vero	true, genuine
verso	toward, near, about
vestito	dress, suit
veterinario	veterinary
vezzo	habit
via	street
viaggio	trip
vicinanza	nearness
vicino	near
vigile	watchful, vigilant, alert
Vigilia di Natale	Christmas Eve
vigna	vineyard
villaggio	village
vincere	to win
vino	wine

viscoso	viscous
viso	face
vivezza	liveliness, vivacity
vivificare	to enliven
vocabolo	word
voglia	wish, desire
volare	to fly
volo	flight
volteggiare	to circle, to vault
vongola	clam
votare	to vote
vuotare	to empty, to drain
vuoto	empty
zia	aunt
zincare	to coat with zinc
zinco	zinc
zio	uncle
zitto	silence
zompare	to jump, to leap
zoo	zoo
zoologia	zoology
zucchero	sugar
zuccheroso	sweet, sugary
zuppa	soup

Appendix B / English to Italian Dictionary

a	un, una
abdomen	addome
accompany, to	accompagnare
acorn	ghianda
act	atto
action	querela
actor	attore
address	indirizzo
advantage	vantaggio
ago	fa
air	aria
airport	aeroporto
alas	ahimè
allowed	lecito
almost	quasi
already	già
also	anche
although	benché, quantunque, sebbene
ambulance	ambulanza
and	e, ed (before vowels)

annoy, to	indispettire
any	qualsiasi, qualunque
apartment	appartamento
appetizers	antipasti
applaud, to	applaudire
apple	mela
appointment	nomina
approve, to	approvare
area code	prefisso
argue, to	litigare
arm	braccio
army	esercito
arrive, to	arrivare
arrow	freccia
as	siccome
at least	almeno
attach, to	agganciare
attempt, to	tentare
attend (to), to	attenersi
attract, to	attirare
audible	udibile
audience	udienza, uditorio
aunt	zia
autumn	autunno
avoid, to	evitare
awake, to be	vegliare
backpack	zaino
bacon	pancetta
bad	malo
bakery	panificio
balance	saldo
ball	palla
bank	banca

banker	banchiere
barber	barbiere
basil	basilico
bathing suit	costume da bagno
bathrobe	accappatoio
bathroom	bagno
bay	baia
bear	orso
beard	barba
beast	bestia
bed	letto
bedroom	camera da letto
beer	birra
begin, to	iniziare
beginners	principianti
bell	campana
belong, to	appartenere
belt	cinta
better	meglio
between	tra
Bible	Bibbia
bill	conto
bind, to	legare
bird	uccello
birthday	compleanno
black	nero
block, to	bloccare
blonde	biondo
blouse	camicetta
blue	azzurro
board, to	salire
boat	barca
book	libro

bookstore	libreria
boredom	noia
boring	noioso, uggioso
both	entrambi
bottle	bottiglia
box	scatola
boy	ragazzo
boycott, to	boicottare
bread	pane
breath	soffio, respiro
bribe	bustarella
bridge	ponte
brother	fratello
brother-in-law	cognato
brown	bruno
bunch	grappolo
bundle together, to	affardellare
but	tranne
butter	burro
button	bottone
by	mediante
calendar	calendario
calm	calmo
can	lattina
carry, to	recare
cashier	cassiere
cat	gatto
cathedral	duomo
cave	caverna, grotto
cellar	cantina
century	secolo
challenge, to	sfidare
channel	canale

chapel	cappella
chat, to	chiacchiere
check	assegno
check, to	controllare
cheer up, to	rallegrare
cheese	formaggio
chest	torace
chicken	pollo
child	bambino
chin	mento
choose, to	scegliere
chop, to	tritare
Christmas	Natale
Christmas Eve	Vigilia di Natale
church	chiesa
circus	circo
citizen	cittadino
city hall	municipio
clam	vongola
classroom	aula, classe
clean, to	pulire
clear	chiaro, lampante
climate	clima
closet	armadio
cloud	nuvola
coat	cappotto
come on	orsù
comic strip	fumetto
coming	entrante
common people	volgo
compel, to	obbligare
complete, to	ultimare
conclude, to	concludere

connection	raccordo
consider, to	reputare
continue, to	perdurare
contract, to	contrarre
cook, to	cucinare
cookie	biscotto
correct	giusto
costly	costoso
cotton	cotone
count	conte
countryside	campagna
cousin	cugino
cow	vacca
cream	crema
credit card	carta di credito
cross, to	varcare
crowd	calca, folla
cup	tazza
cure, to	curare
curse, to	imprecare
customs	dogana
customs agent	doganiere
cut, to	tagliare
dad	papà
daddy	babbo
dairy store	latteria
danger	danno, pericolo
date	dattero
daughter	figlia
daughter-in-law	nuora
dawning	nascente
day after tomorrow	dopodomani
deaf	sordo

debate	dibattito
decade	decenne
deer	cervo
defeat, to	debellare
defect	difetto
deflation	deflazione
democratic	democratico
departure	partenza
deposit, to	depositare
derive, to	provenire
desert	deserto
destiny	destino
destroy, to	distruggere
detour	deviazione
diary	diario
dictionary	dizionario
diet	dieta
directive	direttiva
dirty	sporco
discord	discordia, zizzania
discuss, to	deliberare
discussion	dibattito
dismiss, to	dimettere
distinguished	illustre
disturb, to	turbare
division	reparto
doctor	medico
dog	cane
door	porta
double, to	raddoppiare
down here	quaggiù
down there	laggiù
downstairs	dabbasso

dream	sogno
drink	bibita, bevanda
drug	farmaco
drunk	ubriaco
dry	secco
duck	anatra
during	durante
dust	spolverare
ear	orecchio
earth	terra
east	est, levante
Easter	Pasqua
eat, to	mangiare
egg	uova
elaborate, to	elaborare
elbow	gomito
election	elezione
electrify, to	elettrificare
elevator	ascensore
eliminate, to	eliminare
else	oppure
emergency	emergenza
emotional	emotivo
empty	vuoto
encore	bis
enjoy, to	gradire
enormous	enorme
enter, to	entrare
entire	intero
entrance	ingresso
envelope	busta
epoch	epoca
equator	equatore

erode	erodere
escape, to	eludere, evadere
evening	sera
event	evento
every	ogni
everybody	ognuno
everywhere	dovunque, dappertutto
evil	malo
exact	esatto
exactly	appunto
exactly the same	uguale
excel, to	eccellere, primeggiare
excellent	ottimo
except	eccetto
exceptional	eccezionale
exhibit	mostra
exit	uscita
exotic	esotico
expensive	caro
expert	maestro
explain, to	spiegare
face	viso
face-to-face	quattrocchi
factory	fabbrica, opificio
fail, to	fallire
fall, to	cadere
family	famiglia
famous	famoso
far	lontano
fare	tariffa
fascism	fascismo
fast	rapido
fat	grasso

father	padre
father-in-law	suocero
feel, to	palpare
festival	festa, sagra
fever	febbre
fill (up), to	empire
final	ultimo
find, to	trovare
finger	ditto
finish, to	terminare
fire	fuoco
fireplace	caminetto
first class	prima classe
fish	pesce
fixed	fisso
flight	volo
flood	alluvione
floor	pavimento
flow, to	fluire
fly, to	volare
fog	nebbia
foot	piede
footstool	sgabello
foreign	estero
forest	bosco
fork	forchetta
free	libero
freedom	libertà
freeze, to	gelare
freezing	gelido
frost	gelo
fruit	frutta
frustrate, to	frustrare

fry, to	friggere
full	pieno
future	futuro
gallery	galleria
garden	giardino, orto
garlic	aglio
gate	cancello
get drunk, to	ubriacarsi
ghost	fantasma
gift	dono
giggle, to	ridacchiere
girl	ragazza
give in, to	demordere
glass	vetro
glasses	occhiali
gloves	guanti
go, to	andare
goat	capra
god	dio
goddess	dea
godfather	padrino
godmother	madrina
goldsmith	orafo
grandfather	nonno
grandmother	nonna
grass snake	biscia
grave	tomba
gray	grigio
grease, to	ungere
green	verde
greet, to	salutare
grill	griglia
gross	madornale

ground floor	pianterreno
guess, to	indovinare
habit	tonaca, vezzo
half	metà
hang, to	appendere
happen	capitare
happiness	allegria
happy	allegro
harmful	nocivo
hat	cappello
head	testa
healthy	salubre
heat	caldo
heat, to	riscaldare
heat up, to	scaldarsi
heaven	paradiso
heavy	greve
Hebrew	ebreo
helicopter	elicottero
helmet	elmetto
herb	erba
here	qua, qui
hero	eroe
hide, to	celare, nascondere, occultare
high school	liceo
highway	autostrada
hill	altura, colle
hit, to	battere
holiday	giorno festivo
honest	dabbene
honesty	onestà
honey	miele
horror	orrore

horse	cavallo, equino
hospital	ospitale
hostage	ostaggio
hostel	ostello
howl, to	ululare
humanity	umanità
humor	umore
hunger	fame
hunt, to	braccare
hurricane	uragano
husband	marito
hygiene	igiene
ice cream	gelato
if	qualora
ignore, to	ignorare
illegal	illegale
illicit	illecito
immense	immenso
immigrate, to	immigrare
import, to	importare
improper	improprio
in order that	affinché
inadequate	incongruo
incite, to	incitare
income	reddito
inexpensive	economico
inexperience	imperizia
infinitive	infinitivo
inflate, to	gonfiare
inflation	inflazione
influence	influsso
inn	osteria
inside	dentro

insist, to	insistere
instead	invece
institute	istituto
international	internazionale
intersection	incrocio
invitation	invito
irony	ironia
island	isola
issue	questione
itinerary	itinerario
jacket	giacca
jail	carcere
job	mestiera
joke, to	celiare
journey	tragitto
joy	letizia
jungle	giungla
keep, to	mantenere
key	chiave
kick, to	calciare
kidney	rene
kill, to	uccidere
king	re
kingdom	regno
kiss	bacio
kiss, to	baciare
knife	coltello
lack	mancanza
lake	lago
lamb	agnello
lamp	fanale, lampada
land, to	atterrare
landlord	affittacamere

language	lingua
large	grande
later	in ritardo
learn, to	imparare
leave, to	uscire
leg	gamba
lemon	limone
lend, to	imprestare
lengthen, to	dilungare
less	meno
lesson	lezione
letter	lettera
lettuce	lattuga
library	biblioteca
lie	menzogna
lie down, to	sdraiarsi
light	luce
lightning	fulmine
limit, to	limitare
line	fila
lip	labbro
listen, to	ascoltare, udire
living room	soggiorno
loaf	pagnotta
loan	prestito
lock	lucchetto
look	piglio
look for, to	cercare
look forward to, to	pregustare
lottery	lotteria
love	amore
lung	polmone
machine	macchina

magazine	rivista
magic	magia
mail, to	imbucare, impostare
main	principale
make a reservation, to	prenotare
make lazy, to	impigrire
man	uomo
manager	gestore
market	mercato
marriage	nozze
master	padrone
masterpiece	capolavoro
mattress	materasso
measure, to	misurare
midnight	mezzanotte
mild	mite
milk	latte
mind	mente
mirror	specchio
misfortune	sfortuna
mix, to	mescolare, mischiare
money	denaro, quattrini
money order	vaglia
monster	mostro
monument	monumento
moon	luna
more	più
more than enough	davanzo
morning	mattina
mortgage	ipoteca
mosquito	zanzara
mother	madre
mother-in-law	suocera

mountain	montagna
mouth	bocca
Mr.	signore
Mrs.	signora
mud	fango
museum	museo
mushroom	fungo
musical	musicale
mussel	cozza
mustache	baffi
myth	mito
name	nome
narrative	narrativa
nation	nazione
native language	madrelingua
nature	natura
near	verso, vicino
nearly	quasi
neglected	negletto
neighborhood	quartiere
nephew	nipote
new	novello
New Year's Day	Capodanno
news	notizia
newsstand	edicola
niece	nipote
night	notte
noon	mezzogiorno
north	nord, settentrione
nose	naso
not	non
note	nota
notebook	quaderno

nothing	niente
now	adesso
nude	nudo
nuptial	nuziale
nurse	infermiere
obey, to	ubbidire
object	oggetto
obstruct, to	ostruire
obvious	ovvio
ocean	oceano
offer, to	offrire
official	ufficiale
often	spesso
olive	olio
omit, to	omettere
on top	sopra
one	uno
onion	cipolla
only	solamente, soltanto
open	aprire
opinion	parere
order, to	ordinare
outside	fuori
outstanding	esimio
pacify, to	rabbonire
package	fardello, pacchetto
page	pagina
paint, to	dipingere
painting	quadro
pair	paio
pants	pantaloni
paper	carta
parents	genitori

park	parcheggiare, posteggiare
partner	socio
pass, to	passare
passport	passaporto
past	scorso
pastry shop	pasticceria
pay, to	pagare, sborsare
payment	pagamento
peace	pace
peanut	arachide, nocciolina
pear	pera
pedal	pedale
peninsula	penisola
people	gente
permit	nullaosta
pharmacy	farmacia
phase	fase
piano	pianoforte
piece	pezzo
pill	pillola
pistol	pistola
place	luogo
play, to	giocare
plead, to	perorare
pocket	tasca
poison	veleno
police headquarters	questura
politeness	creanza
Pope	papa
pork	maiale
positive	positivo
postcard	cartolina
potato	patata

praise, to	decantare
pray, to	pregare
prefer, to	preferire
pregnant	incinta, pregno
price	prezzo
pride	orgoglio
priest	sacerdote
primary school	elementari
prime minister	primo ministro
prior event	antefatto
prison	carcere, galera
promise, to	promettere
public place	locale
purple	viola
pursue, to	perseguire
push, to	spingere
put before, to	anteporre
put on, to	mettersi
qualification	qualifica
quantity	quantità
queen	regina
rabbit	coniglio
race	razza
rain	pioggia
rain, to	piovere
raincoat	impermeabile
raise, to	ergere, levare
raspberry	lampone
rat	ratto
read, to	leggere
reality	realtà
reason	motivo
receipt	quietanza, ricevuta

red	rosso
relative	parente
relax, to	rilassare
remain, to	rimanere
repair, to	raccomodare
resemble, to	somigliare
resentment	rancore
reside, to	dimorare
restaurant	ristorante
restore, to	reintegrare, restaurare
result	esito
rhyme	rima
rhythm	ritmo
rich	ricco
right	destra
ring	anello
ring, to	suonare
ritual	rito
river	fiume
rob, to	derubare
robber	predone
robbery	rapina
roll	panino
room	stanza
rope	corda
round	tondo
rule	norma, regola
rumor	fama
sad	triste
safe	sicuro
safety	sicurezza
salary	salario
sale	svendita

same	medesimo
sand	rena, sabbia
schedule	orario
scheme, to	tramare
score	punteggio
sea	mare
seafront	lungomare
secret	segreto
send, to	inviare, mandare
sense of smell	olfatto
several	parecchio
sex	sesso
shade	ombra
shadow	pedinare
sheep	ovino, pecora
sheet	lenzuolo
shellfish	crostaceo
shoe	scarpa
shop	bottega
shout, to	urlare
show	spettacolo
shy	timido
sign, to	firmare
silence	zitto
silent	tacito
sink	lavadino
Sir	signore
sister	sorella
sister-in-law	cognata
ski, to	sciare
skillful	valente
sleep, to	dormire
smile, to	sorridere

snow	neve
snow, to	nevicare
soap	sapone
soccer	calcio
socks	calzini
someone	qualcuno
son	figlio
son-in-law	genero
soup	minestra, zuppa
spring	primavera
stage	palcoscenico
staircase	scala
stamp	bollo
station	stazione
stepbrother, half brother	fratellastro
stepfather	patrigno
stepmother	matrigna
stepsister, half sister	sorellastra
still	ancora, tuttora
stomach	ventre
stop, to	fermare
store	negozio
storm	tempesta
story	racconto
strange	strano
strawberry	fragola
street	strada, via
strike	sciopero
strong	forte, robusto
such	tale
sugar	zucchero
summer	estate
sun	sole

supporter	fautore
surrender	resa
sweat, to	sudore
sweater	maglione
sweet	zuccheroso
swim, to	nuotare
table	tavola
take, to	prendere
take off, to	decollare
tank	serbatoio
taste	gustare
taxes	tasse
telephone	telefono
theater	teatro
therapy	terapia
thief	ladro
thin	magro
thing	faccenda
ticket	biglietto, multa
ticket window	sportello
tie	cravatta
tobacco	tabacco
today	oggi
toilet	gabinetto
tomato	pomodoro
tomorrow	domani
tourist	turista
toward	verso
toy	balocco
tragedy	tragedia
train	allenare, treno
trap	trappola
trip	viaggio

trouble	grattacapo
true	vero
trust	fiducia
turkey	tacchino
turn, to	girare
uncle	zio
under	sotto
unexpected	inatteso
unify, to	unificare
United States	Stati Uniti
universe	universo
university	università
up (here)	quassù
up (there)	lassù
urgent	urgente
used	usato
useful	utile
useless	inutile
usual	solito
vacation	vacanza
vegetable	ortaggio, vegetale
veterinary	veterinario
village	villaggio
vineyard	vigna
vote, to	votare
waiter	cameriere
walk, to	camminare
wall	muraglia, parete
wash oneself, to	lavarsi
watch, to	guardare
water	acqua
wealth	ricchezza
wedding	nozze

weekend	fine settimana
west	occidente, ovest
when	quando
where	ove
white	bianco
wide	largo
width	larghezza
wife	moglie
win, to	vincere
wind	vento
window	finestra
wine	vino
wine bar	enoteca
winter	inverno
without	senza
woman	donna
word	vocabolo
worker	operaio
wrap, to	incartare
wrist	polso
writing desk	scrittoio
year	anno
yellow	giallo
yesterday	ieri
zone	zona
zoo	zoo
zoology	zoologia

Index

W

Y

9 781598 695502